In *Meet them where they're at*, Richard draws on theory and theology, and their interaction with the practice of doing detached work, to present a practical approach to working with those outside of the church. Much of the material comes out of his own experience in Cheltenham where he has given of himself for the sake of the young people. He has shown that incarnational work is godly, costly and unavoidable if we are to make the Christian faith real to this generation of 'pre-non-Christians.'

David Howell
Centre for Youth Ministry (CYM)

I am always most impressed by people who manage to do what they are talking about. Richard shows how to do detached youth ministry in difficult situations, in a way that combines very practical down to earth advice with good theoretical insights. It's a wonderful story of transformation.

Jonny Baker
http://jonnybaker.blogspot.com
National Youth Co-ordinator for Church Missionary Society

In the many gatherings that I have addressed, I spend fifty percent of my time trying to get people in 'the world' to join the church and the other fifty percent trying to get the church to join the world! It is time to get out of our sanctified comfort zones, roll up our sleeves and rediscover God's passion for the world in our heart and actions. This book will help you on the way – go for it!

Dave Wiles
CEO Frontier Youth Trust (FYT)

Meet them where they're at

Meet them where they're at

Helping churches engage young people through detached youth work

Richard Passmore

Additional material by Jo and Nigel Pimlott

SUbtle products are youth publications of

Scripture Union, 207-209 Queensway, Bletchley, MK2 2EB, England

ISBN 1 85999 739 2

British Library Cataloguing-in-Publication Data

A catalogue record for this book is available from the British Library.

Cover design by Martin Lore

Printed and bound in Great Britain by Creative Print and Design, Ebbw Vale

Scripture Union

↳ We are an international Christian charity working with churches in more than 130 countries providing resources to bring the good news about Jesus Christ to children, young people and families - and to encourage them to develop spiritually through the Bible and prayer.

As well as our network of volunteers, staff and associates who run holidays, church-based events and school Christian groups, we produce a wide range of publications and support those who use our resources through training programmes.

Meet them where they're at

Acknowledgements

There are many people to thank, but those who I have learnt most from, are the young people with whom I have worked; Phil and Burnie who I no longer see as young people but as friends. There are hundreds of young people who have shared my journey from time to time and I am thankful to each of them for the privilege of walking alongside them. James Hawes was in my thoughts as together we developed so much of the material for a training manual. His clear thinking and constant challenge to earth youth work theologically and culturally has always been an inspiration. My family have been a tremendous support, helping with early notes and drafts, and even my children Josiah and Bethany helped with the printing of them. Thanks to my co-worker, Phil Colmer, whose natural gifting in relational youth work always put me in his shadow on the street. Also everyone at Cheltenham Youth for Christ between '93 and '98. Finally to Nigel and Jo Pimlott for all their hard work and extra input, Lori and all at FYT for getting the book off the ground and their encouragement and support.

Setting the scene

1 Setting the scene

What on earth was I doing out in this weather? I knew it would be cold but I hadn't reckoned on there being so much rain, or so many young people out in it. The last few weeks had been mild and reasonably dry but the estate had been a ghost town. We had spent several nights seeing only one or two young people we knew, on the way to the chip shop or finishing their paper round, and now it was raining and cold and we were standing chatting to a group of eight or so, shivering outside the chip shop. I'd been chatting to the group for less than five minutes and I wanted to go home.

'Let's go to Al's shop for some crisps,' one young person suggested.

'Great,' I thought, 'shelter'.

I knew Al had a Coca-Cola awning over his door where we could keep out of the rain. By the time we arrived at the shop all the young people had been out in the rain for an hour or so and were soaked. Once at Al's I waited whilst a few of them went in for food.

'Great, OK' I thought, 'I can cope with the cold, because at least I'm dry under here'. At this point I felt water hit my face. I looked up casually and checked that the awning wasn't leaking. There was the water again: I looked around, and none of the young people had water pistols. I soon discovered the source. A new game had been invented. Ryan had discovered his coat was waterlogged, so much so that if he flicked his sleeve, water came out, and what was worse was that his aim was getting better.

'What on earth am I doing out in this weather?' I asked myself again. By the time that joyful thought *flashed through my mind, I discovered I was the only one left under the awning. The other young people had discovered Ryan's new game, and were standing out in the pouring rain to fill up their coats to join in. As if the rain wasn't enough, there soon erupted a water-flicking fight.*

Young people are incredibly inventive and creative. There is no denying young people's creativity, however latent it may be – after all, they are made in the image of God, the ultimate Creator. The negative press about young people will always outweigh the positive and we know that, in the eyes of most news editors, good news is no news, or only worth a 30 second slot at the end, or two inches in the local daily. The truth is that there are still far more positive contributions made by young people to society than negative. It is important for all of us to keep in mind the positives about young people, not just the nice young people who are easy to get on with, but all young people.

Often we think of the estate down the road or on the edge of town as a terrible place. Gossip and the local papers too easily trick us into believing the negative aspects. We need to realise that God is already at work in the community. When I first moved to Cheltenham to be a youthworker we lived on the nice side, amongst the big houses with lots of parks. The area was lovely but no one spoke to us and no one was interested in building relationships. However hard we tried, it didn't work. We even got complaints for putting up a homeless friend for a while. When we moved on to the local housing estate it was like a breath of fresh air. There was life and vibrancy, the neighbours came to say hello and within two weeks we knew more people in our street than in the whole area in which we used to live. There were practical expressions of the kingdom of God from non-Christians that often far outweighed what was seen in church.

Jesus the Word became flesh and lived among us. He became like us in order for us to be like him. For me, detached work is best practised in this way, leading by example. We chose to live on the estate because we felt called to do so. It was a difficult decision to make, particularly when we had a young family. Despite what I said earlier about the good times, there were also difficult times and the personal cost to us was high. Yet I believe it reaped tremendous rewards. Every time I went for a pint of milk or newspaper, I would see young people I knew. There was no pretence of us coming in from the out-side as do-gooders.

> *I will never forget a meeting with residents about the amount of crime on the estate, and one county council worker getting slammed by the residents for suggesting they reported more crime. A mother of four snapped back 'It's OK for you to say that. You go home to your nice cosy house at the end of the day. We get a f*****g brick through the window.'*

Living where you are going to work isn't for everyone but there is a huge drought of Christians living in poorer communities, and often the local churches are struggling and need support. The term often used for this is 'redemption and lift': people become Christians, become more empowered, maybe get jobs and move out of the area. After living on such an estate I can fully understand why, but we do need to question our motives. Is this about a better life for me or for others? Where am I called to be? I remember an old saying going round the church, 'If you are not sure of what you are called to, just go and find a dark place and shine'. It may be clichéd, but it contains tremendous truth and challenge.

There are still far more positive contributions made by young people to society than negative.

Most churches and Christian youth groups around the country do not take up this challenge. Young people are leaving the church in droves, and many children of Christian parents do not want to attend church, let alone invite their friends along. Church based youth work is vital and important, but there are many more young people outside the church than inside. Youth work specialist Pete Ward once said that churches rely too much on young people reaching their friends outside the church youth group, and those friends reaching their friends and so on, which is a fundamentally flawed method of evangelism. It has some obvious value, but will not reach all young people, as most young people mix in groups of like-minded individuals. Pete suggested the maximum number of young people who could be reached in this way would be about 12%, leaving a massive 88% untouched and unreached.

While preparing a talk on the value of detached youth work, I decided to count up how many young people I saw, on one particular evening while out on detached work. Within 40 minutes I had seen over 70 young people I knew well, at which point I stopped counting. I mentioned this in the talk, although I forgot to mention that I also didn't have to heat a hall, replace snooker cues, or buy tuck. I am not suggesting that you undertake detached work because it is cheaper, but we do need to find ways to build relationships with the millions of young people who never get touched by the church in a meaningful way.

Detached work is based on a relational model of youth work. I believe that all youth work should be centred around this way of working. If we were to think this through, and accept it, it would radically challenge our strategies of youth work and mission. Secular youth work agencies know the importance for young people of having appropriate adult relationships, therefore the church should acknowledge this also. It is difficult to deny God's part in relationships as he is where relationship starts, and relationships are the beginning of society; to remove God causes chaos and brokenness. When God created this world he built it on relationships – everything is interconnected – but since the fall, relationships have been in disharmony. Jesus came to bring back harmony and wholeness to the broken relationships, so that they can be reconnected. Through the gospel of Jesus, relationships can be restored and renewed.

To reach young people on the margins of society with this good news, we need to understand that the gospel is holistic, and put this into practice. Justice and righteousness are pillars of our faith, and these principles need to be shown in our work. The church has often swung from one pillar to the other, resulting in an emphasis on 'proclamation' at one end of the theological spectrum, and 'social action' at the other. As youth workers we may often find ourselves working in difficult situations with broken or hurting young people. We cannot do young people or the gospel justice if we have an 'either/or' mindset. The street is often a hard place to be, and to be effective we must see the gospel in a way that will affect every area of our lives. It must affect our lifestyle and how we interact with young people. If they are hungry, we should be willing to feed them, either physically or spiritually. Both are valid expressions of the gospel when shown in love.

When we share the gospel, we must engage in contextual theology. That is, we need to understand the culture we are entering and what the gospel means within that given culture, developing a street spirituality and theology specific to our area. Different issues will be more prevalent in different situations, but we must grapple with the Bible and search for its relevance to our communities, our lives and the lives of the young people we work with. This is vitally important, otherwise the language we use will have little meaning. In the light of this, we must re-examine the words and concepts we use to explain the gospel. In doing so, we will see the reality of God's word, the two edged sword that has power to cut through to the hearts of individuals and situations. (Heb 4:12)

> I remember taking two young people to the Greenbelt festival; we had been working with these guys for a number of years and often talked about God. They had been to church a couple of times but didn't think it was relevant. Over the four days of Greenbelt, we had some great chats about the gospel and the need to make certain choices. They both understood each element of the gospel story: the world being ace, sin spoiling it, Jesus being born, Jesus not sinning, Jesus dying, Jesus taking away sin on the cross and Jesus rising again. The trouble came when we tried to put it all together, added in their response and called it becoming a Christian. They couldn't get their heads around this abstract concept. It was like when my teacher tried to explain algebra to me. In the end, I suggested we forget about the spiritual gymnastics and told them that if they were serious about God, they should walk the prayer labyrinth on the site, think about the individual elements and decide, if they chose to go one hundred percent for God, then they would be Christians. One walked the labyrinth that night, the other the following day.

Their response and choice to start their journey thrilled me. At first I still had questions about why they couldn't put it all together, and why theirs wasn't the neatly packaged gospel conversion you hear about. The more I thought about it, the more I realised that they hadn't just signed into a club but they had chosen to go one hundred percent for God. I realised I would rather have two young people choosing that, than twenty responses to a neatly packaged gospel presentation that people hadn't really thought about.

When we are engaging with young people outside the church, we need to recognise that we are working in a missionary setting. We may not be on the other side of the world but we are working in a different culture, often speaking a different language, with different codes of behaviour, norms and values. I find Bob Mayo's definition of three groups of people a helpful way to see the task set before detached workers in the post-Christian West.

'There are Christians. There are non-Christians and there are pre-non-Christians. Non-Christians are people who have had contact with church or Christians and have some understanding of the framework of Christianity. The reason they are not Christians is hostility, apathy or disagreement. Pre-non-Christians are people who have little or no knowledge or understanding of Christ or Christianity. Jesus is a word to be used negatively, it is nothing more than a swear word. The reason they are not Christians is not hostility, apathy or disagreement and ignorance of the basic Christian stories.'[1]

> As with most things in the Christian faith, detached work is most effectively learnt alongside someone else.

It has been my experience time and time again, as I meet young people on the street, that they are not hostile, but unaware of the authentic gospel story. They are, as Bob Mayo suggests, 'pre-non-Christians.'

This book is an overview of detached work and although it will give some starting points, no book can give you all the skills needed for what is one of the most personally demanding and exciting areas of youth work. As with most things in the Christian faith, detached work is perhaps most effectively learnt alongside someone else.

Throughout this book several key areas will arise, such as principles of communication, non-book learning, observation and relationships. There may be things that you do not agree with, but please take some time to think through them. Ask yourself, 'Why don't I agree with that?' 'Is it crucial that I agree with this?' Ask questions, reflect, raise doubts and work through the issues. The young people you meet will also help challenge your viewpoints if you stick around them long enough.

There are lots of people undertaking detached work or other forms of relational work around the country. In 1995 a conference was called for Christian workers in this field. One of the aims of the conference was to try to bring some definition to the whole area of relational youth work, and people were asked to define the concept. Below are some of the ideas. I hope this will inspire you in your work and challenge you to think again about the nature of youth work.

'Relational youth work is a process.'

'Relational work requires us to take risks, to initiate fresh ventures and to expand our comfort zones.'

'Relational youth work draws directly from the concept of incarnation. In this we regain the excitement of allowing God to enter humanity and transform it. This will be the case for both the workers and the young people to whom they are called.'

'Within relational work we must start from where they are at, not where we would like them to be.'
Relational Youth Work Conference 1995 [2]

Exploring the edges

● In the busy world of activities and high expectations, ask yourself if the balance between activities and relationships in your work with young people is a good one.

● Where would you place yourself on the spectrum between 'proclamation' (evangelism) and 'service' (social action)?

● Is it enough just to demonstrate good news through your actions and who you are?

● What is good news?

● Reflect on the distinctives of the area you live in, from the perspective of a young person.

Detached
work

2 Detached work

I love going hill walking through really rugged terrain, the steeper the better, even more so if you have to scramble over rocks and boulders. The part I really like is the isolation – just you and a mate walking. The best walk I have ever done was Carrauntoohil in Southern Ireland. It was a hot day, we were following a ridge-type route and the views were fantastic. The best thing about that walk was it took over ten hours and we only saw two other walkers and a sheep farmer.

When I started out in detached work in Devon I had a similar experience; I couldn't find many young people. I started in the late summer, when the weather was still ok. The young people were pretty mobile, often moving on from one place to another as they got bored or received 'grief for hanging out in that part of town. As the town was quite spread out most of the young people cycled. On reaching the age of sixteen, a 50cc moped was the thing to get, as buses were few and far between, and on reaching seventeen, the first thing you did was get a car. Consequently, they were often driving around – from the park to the square, up to the school, across to the rec and a few other places in between. I would arrive at the park just in time to be informed by the younger brothers playing on the swings that they had 'gone up the rec'. I would walk there only to discover they had gone to the off licence. They were not trying to avoid me, thankfully, but that was their pattern of behaviour. On a few occasions I thought it might have been more profitable to stand on the main road and jump out in front of them as they drove past. I decided I needed transport, but we didn't have any money. We *thought we'd better do the Christian thing and pray about the situation, and we received an anonymous gift for the right amount of money to buy a motorbike from a friend, who was selling it cheap. Now not only was I able to find the young people before 10 pm, but my street cred went up (just a bit, as the bike was only a 125cc). Once winter set in, I met the young people at a local pub that let them gather there to play pool and use the jukebox.*

Detached work was first seen in Britain back in the sixties. It is a versatile, non-threatening, young-person-centred approach to youth work. It can be highly effective in both urban and rural settings, and is an important tool for reaching young people that the church would not normally come into contact with. The youth worker goes onto the young person's turf – for example pubs, street corners, arcades or cemeteries. As the worker is not responsible for a venue, there is a shift in the power dynamic that allows the worker to be more flexible and responsive to the young people.

Power is an important factor to understand in detached work, as it is in any form of youth work. The traditional idea of power centres on control, primarily the control of others, to bring about change by making others change to our plans and ideas. Often, this it is what happens when the injustice between poor and rich rises to intolerable levels and those without power overthrow those with. Paulo Friere talks about this in *Pedagogy of the Oppressed,*[3] and goes on to explain that often the oppressed become oppressors as they end up using similar tactics to previous authorities, coercing people into changing their ideas and not really bringing about long term change.

How does this affect detached work? Normally, youth work takes place in a building, where the organisation who own the building, and/or the youth worker running the session, is in charge. They hold the power. In detached youth work this is not usually the case. The young person is on their own territory and the balance of power has shifted. Working with young people can either be about change or control (see Chapter 7). As Christians, we should be agents of change; Jesus talked about freedom from control, within a kingdom of life. The exciting thing about our Christian life is that we are on an adventure, even better than a ride at Alton Towers, with more twists and turns than we can imagine. Just like the ride Oblivion, where you dive headlong into a hole in the ground, none of us really know when or how things will end up. We need to give our work with young people the kind of freedom where it can take unexpected twists and turns. That means relinquishing any notions of power we may have and letting the young people set the agenda, arrange the programme or plan the activities. We should put all our security in Jesus, sit back and enjoy the ride.

> We need to give our work with young people the kind of freedom where it can take unexpected twists and turns. That means relinquishing any notions of power.

There are two other types of youth work carried out on the streets that should not be confused with detached work. The first is outreach work (which is different to evangelistic outreach), where a worker operates from a youth centre or club, and aims to bring young people back to this base to continue working with them. They are essentially working in an extended way to contact young people, encouraging them to attend sessions in the club. Often young people end up becoming members and attend regular sessions. Mobile venues, such as buses and caravans, are more readily confused with detached work, as they tend to go where the young people are. Often the workers here will seem to be doing detached work and it can be difficult to draw the line between the two. Generally the difference centres around the responsibility and power dynamic of the worker. If you have young people come to any sort of venue, then as a worker you have to be responsible for that venue, whether it is a mobile project or a purpose-built centre. At some point, a power and authority issue will come into play, regardless of how laid-back you are about material things. If a young person decides to let off the fire extinguisher, or write on the wall, you have to intervene. You may warn them not to do it again, or threaten them with a two week ban. In a detached setting, a worker cannot ban a young person from the park, for example. This is not to say that a detached worker doesn't challenge certain behaviour, but it is done in the context of relationship rather than authority and responsibility.

There has always been detached work happening in various forms within the church, but many projects may not have stated or even realised that this was what they were doing. Frontier Youth Trust (FYT) have a long history of supporting Christians as they try to reach out to more marginalised young people, either through open youth clubs or through detached work. (The FYT conference is an important date in the calendar of those working with young people outside the church.) The growth of Oxford Youth Works and its focus on relational work has also had an impact, and challenged people to think about working with young people outside of those who attend the youth club. In 1995, the first Relational Conference was held, sponsored by Oxford Youth Works, Soul Survivor and Youth for Christ, drawing together many people working relationally with young people outside the church. Over the last few years there has been a steady growth of Christians engaging with young people in their communities through detached work and other forms of relational work. It was encouraging to see so many people attending the detached work seminar at Brainstormers 97, who were either already doing detached work or about to start.

To some, detached work may seem a laid-back job where all you do is chat, eat chips and kick a ball around. There is, however, far more to it than that. It is possible to do the above and call it 'detached work' but like in any sphere of work, there will be good and bad workers. Bearing in mind the power and change issues outlined earlier, it is still important to have some framework for an open canvas. If you aim at nothing, you hit nothing. There are several aims in detached work which are fairly constant, although detailed goals will differ depending on the agency you work for, whether it is Christian work or not, the geographical area and culture you are working in. In the next section, we will look at some general aims, which hopefully allow space for work to develop in diverse settings. These aims have been adapted from the National Youth Agency publication, *Understanding detached work and helping others manage it.*[4]

Aims of detached work

1   **To build relationships with young people who have few positive relationships or avenues for support, and, to help them realise their full potential.**

Detached work often focuses on vulnerable young people, those who hang around on the streets, many because of difficulties at home. For some it may be more extreme than others, having an abusive or alcoholic parent for example. For others it may be a lack of relationship or just not being able to connect with their Dad. There are other young people who don't like the structure of youth clubs, or aren't into watching TV. Regardless of the reason, these young people often don't quite fit, and the reality of today's society means they could be deemed at risk. This further reinforces the need for appropriate adult relationships. The support given can be varied, from information and informal suggestions, to being a listening ear, or supporting a young person through a difficult time. The potential of this to help young people is immense.

I worked with a group of young people in Devon, who met regularly in the pub. A group of six of them wanted to try to establish something more appropriate for young people in the area. They decided that the only way anyone would listen to them was if there were a significant number of them – then their voice would be heard. The group decided to run an event called 'Adults Barred' (I was allowed to attend, as I was only twenty-two). They trawled through various youth work publications for ideas of what people had initiated in other areas. Finally, they whittled the projects down from about sixty to the fifteen they thought most suitable for their area. These fifteen projects were written up and put into a catalogue. A date was set for an 'Adults Barred' event in the back room of a local pub and publicity was sent out around the town and surrounding villages, inviting young people to come and have their say. Due to the rather controversial title of 'Adults Barred', a lot of interest was generated in the media, and the town council were more than a little concerned that the lack of youth provision was getting so much publicity. The day arrived, and the adult TV crew and radio crew was refused entry to the meeting, as were other adults including members of the town council. The meeting was quite well attended by young people. The group leading explained how the meeting had come about, and divided those present into groups to discuss the catalogue of project ideas. The most appropriate was chosen, and then other issues were discussed. The young people agreed that an informal venue was needed where they were free to come and go, such as a coffee bar. They also supported the proposal that young people in the area needed a youth worker. After the meeting, the core group were interviewed by the press, and the town council called a meeting to take the issue further. Several of the group attended this meeting, where the town council agreed to fund a working party to produce a report on youth work in the area. The report was successful, with a youth worker being appointed and a new management committee put in place at the local youth centre. The centre, which was run down and neglected, was repaired with the help of young people and staffed through volunteers. The young people achieved an immense amount through this project and also realised that they had potential both as individuals and as a group to make a difference in their lives and the lives of others.

2 To help bridge gaps in understanding between the local community and young people.

Much of the hassle young people are given occurs because of misrepresentation. Often young people who hang out on the corner and are visible to the community are scapegoated for all the problems in the area. Part of a worker's role is to dispel these myths, and help both sides gain a better understanding of each other. This was the role I found myself playing at the meeting called by the town council in response to the 'Adults Barred' event.

3 To identify the needs and interests of young people, and develop appropriate strategies for action, either by the detached team or with other agencies.

This is a general aim, and the project may already be set up to facilitate a particular need. It is important to consider here the needs and interests as determined by the young people themselves: not what we think they need, but what they think they need. This may be the source of the misconception that detached workers have an easy life, as interests of young people often centre around sports and trips. There is no denying that a sunny day out at Alton Towers with a group of young people is a great way to pass the time, and being paid for it may be an added bonus. The important aspect of such a trip is the process leading up to it. We need to provide the right level of support (see section on scaffolding in Chapter Six) to help young people learn through the process of planning the activity.

One lad we worked with had hardly ever used the telephone, so requesting the number from directory enquiries and then phoning the park was a major challenge for him. It took three days of support and encouragement to get him into the office to use the phone, and an hour or so of coaching before he was confident enough in what to say to pick up the phone and call. Then we needed to remind him to say please and thank you, so we didn't put the park off the idea of us visiting.

4 To enable young people to take more control over their lives.

Young people often feel that other people – parents, Social Services and teachers – are running their lives. They can be restricted in many ways, such as lack of transport, money, age, height etc. An important aspect of the worker's role is to empower them to take responsibility for their own lives. For example young people need to recognise the control that a legal or illegal substance may have over them, or if they are being manipulated by others.

> *'Train a child in the way he should go, and when he is old he will not turn from it.'*
> Proverbs 22:6

The emphasis in this passage is on the child, and not on the way, train a child in the way he should go, not in the way you think he should go. I wonder if, young people reject the idea of handing over their life to Jesus because they haven't yet discovered it is their life to live as they see fit.

5 To take good news to those young people that the church would not normally come into contact with.

If, as Pete Ward suggests, 88% of young people will not be reached by traditional methods of youth evangelism, it is vital that the church moves from a complacent maintenance mindset, to being a dynamic missionary organisation which impacts the world around it, beginning a hundred yards down the road. As we have discussed, the gospel is holistic, necessitating social action as well as proclamation. In the nineties, Youth for Christ stated the need for their organisation to move towards a more authentic view of evangelism. They set this out in the four D's.[5]

> *'From 2D evangelism to 4D evangelism.*
> *God has called us to an evangelistic work among young people. We believe that the biblical pattern of that work is not just the opportunity to proclaim good news and for a young person to make a 'decision' for Christ. The strategy is one where we seek to develop the following four dimensions of evangelism that we believe are found in Scripture:*

Demonstrate – the incarnational nature of evangelism – to be where young people are; to love unconditionally and to serve; to be the people of God; to be living sacrifices. Demonstration involves service and suffering, works and wonders, if it is to fully reflect the breadth of good news.

Declare – the proclamation of truth through word and deed. Explaining good news in a culturally relevant way; seeking every phrase and gesture to enable the spiritual link to be made between Christ and the young person.

Decide – the summoning of young people to follow Jesus. The young person has to choose, under the inspiration of the Holy Spirit, to commit their life to Christ. The evangelist is used as a catalyst in this divine-human interaction of salvation.

Disciple – working in partnership with local churches and youth leaders to enable young people to cross the gulf between the jungle of youth culture and the church.'

This is one of the simplest ways of looking at this complex subject and still has much to say to the church in the 21st century. To think in terms of 4D evangelism is helpful and quickly reinforces the gospel's holistic nature. It must be recognised that the four D's do not present a process to work through, but are circular and ongoing within the context of relationships with young people.

Detached work is a long-term approach to working with young people. It takes time to build real relationships. You sometimes think you've built a close relationship quickly on the street, but often these young people have been let down many times before by adults, and only time can cement the relationship. A detached project should have an unlimited life span, as making contacts gets easier the longer you are around. The young people introduce you to their younger brothers and sisters, and you become accepted as part of the community. Churches often have a history of short-term forays into the community. This damages the reputation of Jesus. For a detached work project, people should be looking ten to fifteen years down the line, with individual workers being involved for at least four years, and new workers coming alongside to work with them before the baton is passed to them. The exception to this can be when a project is initiated or started with the specific aim of leading to something else. It may require a short-term, research-based worker who serves for a number of months as the catalyst to get things going, and then passes the project on to others. The important issue with this type of work is that the young people are made fully aware of the nature of the post, and that there are appropriate structures put in place to ensure the project achieves its aim.

Detached workers are increasingly based in schools, and this often happens as an extension of detached work in the community of which the school is a part.

I remember the first time that Phil Colmer, who worked with me in Cheltenham, went into the local school as a detached worker after doing detached work on the local estate for a couple of years. He came back to the office and stated 'I hit the jackpot! I went into a tutorial to introduce myself, and there were seven or so young people I already knew who asked me, "Oi! Phil, what you doing 'ere?"' They met him at lunchtime, and showed him all the places they hung out, which they thought the teachers didn't know about – the modern day equivalent to the back of the bike sheds.

In this case we hoped going into the school would strengthen the relationships, which it did, but it also meant a lot of fresh contacts were made, preparing the way for when we started work in other areas. Phil was in the school to form positive relationships with the young people, on a different level to the teacher-pupil relationship. He was to be a positive role model the pupils could identify with, and with whom they could share their problems, aspirations and dreams. He was not there as a school counsellor or as an authoritative figure.

Detached work can also work well in rural settings. The young people are not as anonymous as they are in towns and cities, so it can be a bit of a challenge finding where they hang out, as they tend to go where adults can't see them. Different ways of doing detached work need to be explored in rural areas, such as travelling on the school bus or being around the bus shelter. Young people in rural communities face many of the same issues faced by young people in urban settings and so the aims are fundamentally the same. However, in rural settings there is also a whole set of difficult issues – a lack of public transport, more limited employment opportunities, isolation, increased parental control due to lack of transport, visibility, and housing, to name but a few. Detached work in rural areas is often vital due to the lack of youth provision, and more work is required by churches to meet the specific needs of these young people.

Exploring the edges

● How 'powerful' are you and in what ways do you exert that power over others?

● How long can you commit to young people through a detached work project? If it is less than five years, will you cause more harm than good in the long run?

● Do you want to ride the 'roller coaster' and what will the implications for you, your church and your family be?

● What are/will be the aims of your detached work project?

● Take time to discuss these issues with your family and friends, and consider the implications detached youth work will have on you. Are others willing to support you and do they have any concerns about you undertaking this type of work?

Differing ideals

3 Differing ideals

*We had been working with Jim for a number of years.
Ever since we had known him, both he and his older
brother had always been in trouble with the police.
On several occasions they had mentioned things they
had done, whether nicking lawnmowers or stealing
from cars. No matter how we challenged them, they
would return to the buzz that crime gave them. On
one occasion we were at the local car park when Jim
came down on a stolen motorbike. It wasn't freshly
stolen, but had been acquired by dubious means
some time ago. As workers we didn't want to reject
Jim but couldn't be seen to be condoning him riding
stolen motorbikes. Jim had come down to show off
the bike to the other young people, and also knew
that I was into motorbikes. We explained that we
couldn't hang around whilst he was on the bike, but
would come back later to see if he was OK and have
a chat. When we returned later Jim gave us a
mouthful of abuse about not trusting him, how he
hadn't stolen the bike but bought it. I knew this was
true, but we both also knew the bike was stolen. Jim
couldn't see that what he was doing was wrong, as
he had paid for the bike. The illegality of the issue was
clear, but in Jim's mind everyone did it, so why
shouldn't he? Besides, he was nearly fifteen and he
could legally ride a bike at sixteen anyway – what
was a few months?*

When we get to know young people through detached
work we soon realise that there is a big difference
between our expectations and values and theirs. It
often comes down to the basics of right and wrong.
Young people inhabit the same world but may seem
on a different planet. Theirs is a different culture, a

different language with different norms and values. What is more confusing is that groups of young people can differ from one area of the town to another, from north to south, rural to urban, male to female, black to white. The good news for Christians is that we are not called to see young people as a group, but to love them as the unique individuals God created them to be.

It is important to have some idea of the planet young people inhabit. Many people accept that there is no one dominant youth culture, but that it is made up of many different subcultures. This is easily identifiable when we look at the different groups and cliques young people form. There are skaters, boarders, young people who group around a particular sport, clubbers, the lads, the in crowd and the out crowd. The list could go on. Walk down the street and see who's who in your area.

Youth culture does not stay static. For that matter neither does culture in the Western world. The pace of cultural change is greater now than ever before. Recent times have seen dramatic changes. It has been said that society is undergoing or has undergone (according to who you read) a cultural shift from modernity to postmodernity. Postmodernity at its simplest means that the Western world is changing to be more subjective and less absolute.

The cultural trends and worldviews of modernity were shaped by science and progress. Major figures like Darwin and Newton left their mark. There were tremendous advances in all the scientific fields. If you couldn't prove it, it was not true. The authority of the Bible and its inerrancy came into question.

The rise of postmodernity marked a change in this. People became disillusioned with science, believing that you can't prove everything empirically. There was a growing openness to spirituality, alternative therapies and New Age spiritualities, marked by the popularity of programmes like *The X-Files* and the interest in fantasy and science fiction. Choice and tolerance of different viewpoints became more widespread – 'If it works for you that's fine, go ahead' – was the underlying value base. No one seems to know when postmodernity started, but it was 'Generation X' (this is used to describe the generation born between the mid-sixties and mid seventies) that was growing up in the midst of this huge cultural shift. Since the fifties there have been major changes taking place in society.

The fifties saw the post war boom where, Britain had 'never had it so good'. Then came the swinging optimism of the sixties, closely followed by the unemployment and discontentment of the seventies. In the eighties it was everyone for themselves and Margaret Thatcher declared that 'There is no such thing as society'.[6] One term used to describe the nineties was the 'caring and sharing nineties', but my experience of how our society treats its young, old and most vulnerable doesn't match that statement yet. The generation following Generation X should perhaps have been called Generation Y, but I prefer to use the more common term, 'Millennials'. Born in the eighties and early nineties, these are the teenagers and young people we are working with now.

> We must do as Jesus did, enter into their world and try to understand and experience it.

When we look back at this cultural shift and the fast changing world we live in, it's no wonder that young people seem to be on a different planet. Therefore, we must do as Jesus did, enter into their world and try to understand and experience it.

In the *Future Trends in Youth Ministry* report [7], Rick Bartlett identified eight key issues to consider when working with young people in the future.

1 *Consumerism as the essence of youth culture.*
 Western young people live to consume. Image is everything.

2 *The changing family and it's impact on young people.*
 This group are more valued and cared for than past generations. Parents will be much more protective of their children.

3 *The way technology has transformed youth culture in the last fifteen years.*
 These kids will never know life without CD players, computers, or the Internet. Cyberspace will be the new frontier.

4 *Globalism.*
 Young people have more in common with their peers around the globe than with adults of their own culture.

5 *Tribalism.*
 The opposite of Globalism, the need to make a name for themselves in their local situation.

6   *The erosion of moral values – right from wrong.*
    The marketplace mentality, that makes saying 'this is wrong' almost impossible.

7   *Incarnational youth work.*
    The new generation of young people require cross-cultural ministry.

8   *Openness to the supernatural/spiritual.*
    Young people are asking questions about the supernatural world.

There are more differences that need to be kept in mind. The story about Jim (the guy with the motorbike) contains many elements which are characteristics of the millennial generation. The huge shock I had when starting to work with marginalised young people was that of class difference. Distinctions between middle class and working class often appear to have merged in recent decades but detached workers in poorer communities find themselves working with those whom this process has not affected. As one of the aims in detached work is to bridge the gap between young people and the community, it is important to take into account where the community may be coming from. A study, by the Evangelical Urban Training Project, identifies several differences between middle and working class thought and ways of being. Although they are broad generalisations, and there are many other factors involved, they can be helpful in increasing our understanding of these issues.[8]

Working class		Middle class
Descriptive	*rather than*	Analytical
More sensitive to content		More sensitive to structure
Stress on the active		Stress on the passive
Words convey concrete		Words convey abstract
Reality, feelings		Ideas, concepts and generalisations
Group		Individual
Immobile		Mobile
Present		Future
Splash out		Save
Action		Theory
Wage/Giro		Monthly salary
Feelings		Thoughts
Stories		Books
Generalisations		Concrete examples
Nuclear family		Extended family
Body language		Words
Exaggerated		Understated
Patterned		Linear
Relationships		Rules
Faith and politics		Faith and science
Acceptance		Judgementalism
Openness		Privacy
Vulnerability		Stiff upper lip
Feelings		Facts
Meeting		Meetings

Whether we like it or not we are all shaped by the world around us. The way we think and act is often determined, either consciously or subconsciously, by how the people around us act. My son occasionally mimics his mum. It could be the way he looks at his sister, a mannerism or a phrase. My wife usually bursts into laughter. As Christians we try not to be shaped by the negative things around us, those things we may see as being inappropriate. They can be all sorts of things from swearing, to violence to more subtle things like succumbing to advertisements. It is easy to spot how these outside influences shape us as individuals, but we may not recognise how our local church and view on Christianity is shaped by the dominant issues in today's society, such as consumerism, materialism and the pressure to be productive.

For example, in *Growing up Evangelical,*[9] Pete Ward suggests that, for many of us, songs influence the shaping of our theology. This is not a problem in itself but it can lead to an unbalanced theology. Many of the young people I know are confused by this and believe that the words to all songs are in the Bible somewhere. In small group work, a young person has often quoted the words of a song as if it were Biblical truth. Whilst there is usually consistency between what a songwriter may say and what the Bible says, there is often little consistency in the range of topics these songs focus on.

> If the major influence on our theology comes from the songs we sing, we will not see the picture as God sees it.

There are few songs about how our materialism impacts the poor, how our sexual thought patterns and actions conflict with the holiness of God or how our selfishness and competitiveness damages our peers. These are major biblical themes which are not addressed in song. Consequently, if the major influence (for some, perhaps the only one) on our theology comes from the songs we sing, we will not see the picture as God sees it. Our view of Christianity will thus be distorted. As youth workers we need to know why we believe what we believe in order to authentically pass on the gospel in this postmodern age.

Another influence that has shaped the church has been the dominance of the middle class in British church life. Many assumptions about what is right and proper in church and what is 'Christian' often have far more to do with middle class values than biblical ones.

I remember going to church with a friend, who wasn't a Christian. The preacher was in full flow, when my friend stuck his hand up. The preacher noticed but didn't respond immediately. After a while my friend said 'Excuse me, may I ask question?' After the initial shock, she said, 'Of course you can' and dealt with the interruption quite well. There was silence in the congregation – it was great. The best thing was that for my friend, it was the most normal thing in the world for him to do.

Where does the idea of not smoking in church come from? I know it is a health risk, a fire hazard and addictive, but we serve coffee after the service. Close examination of Scripture doesn't reveal much on the subject. People tend to use the verse about the body being a temple of the Holy Spirit when asked by young people 'where does it say in the Bible you shouldn't smoke?' but I am unsure of the context for this. Shouldn't we be able to give clear answers and distinguish between Biblical truth and accepted practice?

The church is littered with middle class people who know the words of the Bible but don't apply them. Let me give you an example. Do you know that it says in the Bible 'Do not be proud' and 'Fear not for I am with you'. How many of us, however, are not proud, and do not fear? Often Christians have little sayings that, when put to the test are not upheld. For example, Christians often say that 'all sin is the same' yet it can seem that sexual sin is considered far higher on the list than pilfering from the office supplies. For young people going through adolescence this is not helpful. How many issues do we need to get our heads around if we are to do justice to young people and the God we serve?

Some years ago, I did a study with a youth group on the theme of church. We looked at why many of the youth group didn't go to our rather traditional, local Anglican church. We looked at what the Bible said on meeting together. We tried to form some idea of what should happen in church, right from the welcome received at the door, to the relevance of what was said, the acceptance the young people felt and what they thought the role of the vicar should be. After a couple of weeks they had a picture of what they thought a culturally relevant, biblical church should be like, and what form and feeling a service should take. They all attended church the next Sunday to compare their findings with the reality. They walked in, with notebooks, and scored each section out of ten. They all sat at the front and scribbled away during the service, paying real attention to the sermon, even taking notes. After the service they challenged the vicar with their findings. One of the areas the young people found the biggest problem was how unwelcome they felt. Hardly any of the adults spoke to them, some questioned why were they writing in church, and thought they were being rude. The vicar suggested that they give out the hymnbooks next Sunday to help the situation. 'Greeeaaat' said one young person sarcastically. I was a little embarrassed by this, but the group agreed to give it a go. Before the next Sunday a plan was hatched. It was obvious many of the 'olds' didn't want to know, so the group decided to give each adult a warm, big hug as they walked through the door, preferably two hugs by two different young people, hugging them again as they left the church. It was pandemonium. The young people wouldn't let the adults in without being hugged. The adults who tried to sneak around the side, were sprung upon by George hiding by the organ! At the end of the service people were more open to the idea.

Culture is shifting fast for young people. We need to meet these young people where they are. We need to love them unconditionally in the scandalous way Jesus did, care with relentless tenderness, and get involved in the mess of the world around them.

Exploring the edges

● How far do you agree with the following statements? Score yourself according to this scale:

1 = I agree strongly   5 = I do not agree

1	Sex before marriage is wrong.	1 2 3 4 5
2	Youth workers should hand out condoms.	1 2 3 4 5
3	Soft drugs should be legalised.	1 2 3 4 5
4	All drugs are bad.	1 2 3 4 5
5	I would allow young people to verbally abuse me.	1 2 3 4 5
6	The Gospel is always good news.	1 2 3 4 5
7	Violence can be used in a healthy way.	1 2 3 4 5
8	Swearing and offensive language offend me.	1 2 3 4 5
9	It is wrong to be homosexual.	1 2 3 4 5
10	I would receive stolen goods as a 'thank you' present.	1 2 3 4 5
11	Censorship of films and videos is outdated.	1 2 3 4 5
12	All sins are the same in God's eyes.	1 2 3 4 5

● Why did you answer the way you did? Discuss the answers with a
friend who isn't a Christian.

● Do you think the answers would be the same for the young
people you work with?

● Ask a young person to score themselves on this exercise, and
compare their answers to yours.

Getting
started

4 Getting started

Church relations

Detached work is still a relatively unknown phenomenon in churches, and as mentioned, it needs to be long term. Therefore it is essential that the right groundwork is undertaken to prepare yourself, your co-workers, and your church or sponsoring agency before you start.

It is essential that your church gains the correct perspective on what you are trying do. This may mean that you need to talk to people time and time again before they understand. After five years in Cheltenham, people still had difficulty in grasping what we were trying to achieve.

Justin Groves, Diocesan Youth Office for Gloucestershire wrote a paper, called *Unchurching the churched*,[10] outlining the need for people to understand the world in which we live. He identified that there was a need to break out of the Christian subculture, where life becomes insular and people get sucked into a pattern of church activities, and end up seeing themselves as defined by what they do, rather than who they are in Christ. Detached work is a process, just like education. Educating those around you to understand your work will take time.

Start with a small group who are willing to support you and ask them to be advocates for what you are trying to achieve and how you are going about it. Give them all the information you can and encourage them to read around the subject, perhaps you could use the study questions at the end of each chapter with them. One of the most vital things to do is to challenge people's expectations but at the same time set realistic goals and explain how long term the results will be. Be sure to know where you are going with the young people (see later in this chapter). Ministers and congregations will often give a positive gut reaction, as anything to increase numbers in church is welcome. But false expectations can be harmful to the future of the project and need to be challenged sensitively but purposefully. It is unlikely the young people will attend the current church services – due to cultural differences, and the fact they may not wish to attend. This does of course depend on the young people you are contacting.

Thinking of the work in a missionary context is helpful. Missionaries need to build churches that are relevant to the people they are contacting, in the language of the culture in which they are working. Use this example and explain that discipling marginalised young people has more in common with this than it does with traditional youth work. Change doesn't happen overnight.

It has been noted, in more than one church, that difficulties can arise in employing a youth worker to reach out into the community. These difficulties are often only realised as young people from the community start to attend the youth club. The language of the young people is different from that of the church young people and church youth can pick up some of this. Christian parents may notice the different atmosphere and complain about what is going on. If the funding for the club comes from parents who want something to entertain their children, they can feel that they have rights over what happens there. The church leader may want to use the club to reach out, but trying to amalgamate these two different objectives can end in chaos. I have witnessed this situation occur regularly in local churches. Churches should be encouraged to see detached work running in parallel to existing work: a project that runs alongside what is happening in the church, with their full support, but that doesn't necessarily cross over at any point, pre- or post-conversion.

At this point we should mention the current phenomenon of youth churches and congregations. There are several ways of looking at this subject, and there are books and articles which will do the subject more justice than I can. The views of people in your church will be many and varied and, as it often depends on the denomination you are from, I try to adopt a practical approach – if the young people don't fit, why try to make them? If the church is praying for revival, do so in faith that the place will be flooded, then you can have more than one service on a Sunday. Then it will not be a problem to have a youth focused service. There is also a chance that the young people do not want a youth church, and anyway, what constitutes church for young people today? By the time you can answer the last question you may be two years into your project!

It can be helpful to ask questions when engaging in the education process in preparation for a project. There is no point asking questions that can easily be answered. Some that need to be asked are: how did Jesus share his message? Why are we so concerned with numbers when Jesus' initial work was with just twelve? When did the disciples become Christians? How do you do Bible studies with a young person who doesn't read? People may well ask why you question so much, and questioning may be contrary to the predominant culture of your church, but this process is important and worthwhile; trust your questions.

Finally agree on lines of accountability, ensure those you are accountable to understand what you are trying to achieve and keep a written record of it. You should remind each other of what was agreed at least annually, and after any major incidents.

> How do you do Bible studies with a young person who doesn't read?

Ground work

We had recently moved into the area, had only just finished our surveillance and started on some cold contact. We had done two sessions so far – on a Tuesday and Thursday. On one of these evenings we met two lads and introduced ourselves whilst playing frisbee. During the other session we had chatted to a group of four girls and two boys in the same park. This evening I was due to attend a prayer meeting at a local church on the estate. As I walked through the door I was greeted with the words, "You're still alive then?' from a lady called Mary. Thinking she was referring to the reputation of the young people, I explained that they weren't that bad. She replied 'I'm not talking about the young people, you nearly had a visit from a bloke with a shotgun.' I really didn't have a clue what she was talking about. She was genuinely relieved to see that my intestines hadn't been plastered all over the hall late on Thursday night. It transpired that one of the younger girls we had met as part of the

Thursday group had mentioned to her father that they had met two men in the park who were youth workers. He had missed the information that we were youth workers, but caught onto the fact that I lived in the area and had been in the park late in the evening. The daughter mentioned we had said we worked with Youth for Christ which didn't really help, as he thought we were a dodgy American cult. He flipped his lid, and was all for coming around and blowing my brains out, according to Mary. Thankfully his girlfriend got him to ring Mary to see if she knew who we were as she went to church. Fortunately, Mary had remembered who we were, and knew that we would not contact girls without boys or a female worker present. She explained this to the irate father, the daughter explained there were some lads with them, and I lived to tell the tale.

If you want the project to be successful and wish to ensure the safety of yourself and other workers you must undertake a lot of ground work within the community. In today's climate of red tape and bureaucracy, certain aspects may seem to be a waste of time and irrelevant to what you are trying to achieve. It is important, however, to approach the project professionally and pay attention to detail. Your foundations must be right if you want your house to last.

There are differing ideas on where to begin, but it is probably easiest to start by building up a profile of the community in which you hope to work. This should enable you to introduce yourself to the relevant people and assess whether it is really right for you to start work in the area. There may well be some information already written, in which case you can tailor it to your requirements – check with local schools, colleges, charities and councils. Community is a hard word to define. It can be viewed as having two elements:

Community – a group of people living in one geographical area, or
Community – a group of people having cultural, ethnic or other characteristics in common.

For the purpose of building up a profile of the area you hope to work in, it is best to look at the subject this way and differentiate between the two. Whilst detached work can be aimed at specific people groups it is, more often than not, about working with young people in a particular geographical community.

Defining the geographical boundaries of a community can be difficult. Sometimes a railway line or main road may split a community that is thought of as one. It can be helpful to look at a street map and draw where you think the boundary is and then ask others. Targeting your area to begin with is important as it focuses your attention and means that you become known in that area. Once the work is established the boundaries exist less and less as relationships are built. If the proposed area is quite small it may be helpful to have another area close by, to start with, where you can go to meet young people if there is no one around within your area. This will then give you more flexibility for working, and can all be included in one local profile.

The example below shows how one group of detached workers subdivided their area into two patches along a major road that ran through the housing estate they lived on. The area marked 'A' was where they concentrated most of their efforts, whilst the area marked 'B' was where they would occasionally meet young people. This example also gives an idea of how to select boundaries. In this case, the boundaries are roads.

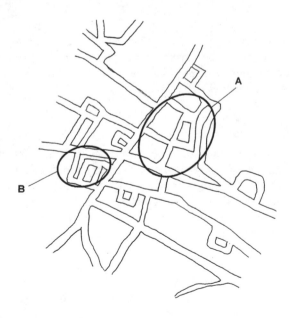

It is important at the start to define your area, but don't set it in concrete. It may well be that as you delve deeper and talk to people, boundaries need to be moved – either extended or made smaller. Once you have done this there are several factors you need to look into.

Location

Find out how your area relates to the rest of the district. Which local authority does it come under? Is it viewed as part of the town or an area in its own right? What does the area border and what effect does this have on the area?

Landscape

What is the area like? Is it set in the middle of an industrial estate? Are there lots of green spaces? Where are the likely areas that young people will congregate?

History

This can be very important, as it often gives a lot of clues as to why certain things happen or particular attitudes are held. Talk to older residents about the area. Find out what was there before. When did the area start to look like it does today?

Population

The best way to find out about this is through the census breakdowns for smaller areas. Often the local council will have already analysed them. Work out how many young people in your target range live in the area. These figures may also give you details on the percentage of people married, ethnic minorities, average number per household and the density of the population.

Housing

Observe the type of housing in the area. Are many derelict, or empty?

Check how many are council houses and how many are privately owned. How does the housing in this area compare to areas close by?

Education

Look at primary, secondary and further education, regardless of the age range you hope to work with. Try to visit the schools and speak to the teachers. See if there are homework clubs in the area and find out who runs them. Try to assess people's attitudes towards education either by talking to them or looking at adult education classes attended locally by people from the estate.

Employment/unemployment

Ask for statistics from local employment agencies. Try to find out more detailed figures for your area. How many males are employed relative to the number of females and why? What is the ratio of people working part time? How many young people are working? Do young people under 16 have jobs? Who are the main employers in the area? Who is most likely to employ a young person from school?

Facilities and youth provision

Are the facilities such as shops centralised in your area or are they outside the area? Find out about the commercial facilities, such as pubs and shops, and look into their attitude towards young people. What are the community facilities in the area: swimming pools, sport halls, libraries, job centres, facilities for the elderly? Are the schools open in the evenings? Research all the youth activities and organisations available to young people and visit them. Do the scout and guide movements attract local young people? Relate the figure to your census details to try to ascertain how many young people attend the current provision. If they don't, why not, and where are they? What is the statutory youth service doing in the area? Who are the face to face workers and who is responsible? What is their strategy for young people in the area?

Transport

Get the local bus or rail timetables. Look at the cost, destinations and regularity and assess their effect on young people in the area. Do parents own cars? How many young people ride motorbikes or have cars?

Other things to look into include local attitudes, health and welfare issues, social services, crime figures etc.

As detached work is long-term and needs to be sustained, it is important to recognise the limitations you and your church may have, either financially or time-wise. Throughout the profile it is wise to bear this in mind and look for other agencies or churches that can support the project. Breaking down these denominational barriers may mean the project's life span and effectiveness is far greater, and there is far less likelihood of the young people being let down because the project cannot be sustained. Joshua and Caleb researched the promised land before they entered it, (Joshua 1) therefore we must assess our situation before we start. It may be that detached work is not appropriate for the area at all.

It is also important to take a more informal look at the neighbourhood. Two ingredients are important when doing this: to walk the area and to use all your senses. Walking the area gives you a very different feel to driving. Walking enables you to use your senses more and takes more time so you naturally see and sense more. Explore where all the alleyways lead, being careful not to trespass. Look at graffiti in the area, remember names. Get some chips to eat in the park for a while to see what is going on, check around for signs of drugs or alcohol. Locate all the post boxes, use the local shops, and read the local papers. Walk a dog, and go where other dog walkers go. Notice the different sights and sounds of the area. Remember, God is already at work in the community. Find out what he is doing and discover where you fit into that. Whilst in Cheltenham, I had the opportunity to do that.

> Cheltenham is set in a valley. The estate we lived on had hills on two sides, one which formed part of the Cotswold Way and was quite beautiful. I would regularly look to these hills and be inspired with fresh hope. One evening, we were chatting to two lads in the park. There was a set of six tyre swings that were arranged together in a hexagonal shape. Usually the local young people would play a game of 'kick and shove'

where the object was to try to kick the tyre out from under whoever you could reach. It was a great place to hang out and, as the tyres all looked in on each other, it was a good place to chat. The evening in question was too mellow to play kick and shove so we just chatted. The lads talked about their day and then asked me what I had been doing. I explained that I had been to a prayer meeting and done some other stuff in the office. They picked up on the prayer meeting and asked what I had done at it. I explained we had talked to God and had waited for God to speak to us. This threw them somewhat, but they weren't fazed and asked how God spoke to us. I could sense this was a special conversation – it doesn't happen very often and I thought my best bet was to just say exactly what had happened at the prayer meeting. I told them about a couple of bits from the Bible that were read out. Then I stuck my neck out and told them that sometimes people see pictures in their mind that might mean something from God, and that one of my co-workers had shared a picture. I explained the picture was about five speedboats, but before I could explain what I thought the picture meant, one of the lads interrupted saying he knew what it was about. I asked him what he thought it meant and he explained it in the same way that we had interpreted it at the prayer meeting. His friend was as shocked as I was and asked about other ways God spoke. I said that God sometimes spoke through other people and the world around us and told him to look at the hills. As he did so, I saw the closest thing I have ever seen to a Damascus Road experience. He had lived in the shadow of these hills all his life, yet as he looked up, it was as if scales fell from his eyes, he heaved a huge breath and said, 'Yeah it's a f****ing miracle'. It was as if he was seeing the hills for the first time because he realised the power behind the creation of them. God was obviously at work in this lad but it was another two years before he became a Christian.

Once you have assessed your area, know it quite well, have spoken to the local authorities, negotiated with your church and got their backing, ask yourself if you really need to do detached work in this area. If you do, work out any relevant policies and procedures, (see chapter 9) and make sure all those working with you are aware of these. Secondly ensure you are fulfilling your legal obligations to work with young people, eg police screening (see chapter 9). Thirdly make some sort of identification card for each member of the team, with their name and picture on it, and a reference telephone number. Log a copy of these with the local police station along with an approximation of when and who will be out. You should already know the community officer for the area, who you should have met whilst undertaking your community profile.

The final question to ask before you start is – where do you hope the detached work will lead? Is it planned as a project in its own right with the work restricted to the streets, or is it leading towards establishing a discipleship group or youth church of some form? What will show that you have achieved your aim? It may be that at this stage you are open-ended, and that is OK – as I have said it can be a roller coaster ride.

Surveillance

We used to say we were the male equivalent of Cagney and Lacey on a stakeout. To start with, we would drive around the estate. This helped us understand where we were going, although several times we would end up down a cul-de-sac and have to turn around and go back the way we had come. The roads seemed like a warren at first. We would be lost for a while, then see something familiar, and realise we weren't lost at all. One of us would drive, the other would observe. There seemed to be so much going on we felt we'd never remember it all. We invested in some hi-tec surveillance equipment – the cheapest dictaphone we could find. It was great if you played around with the speed settings; you could sound like Mickey Mouse on helium. The purpose, however, was to record the goings-on as we drove around, which we later transcribed onto paper.

Now you have a community profile, the next step is to identify the young people you hope to work with, and where and when they hang around. The profile should have given you some starting points, but you need now to build up a view of the habits of the young people. This is the point when you resort to the Cagney and Lacey approach. For example, your profile suggests that the majority of young people from the estate attend school, and hang around in the evenings. Start going out on different evenings, at different times. For example, one week you might start after school and stay for a few hours, then the following week start at 9 pm and stay until after midnight. Keep a note of who is out when, and you will soon notice a pattern in where and when the young people come out. Once you see a group, come back at the same time (more or less) and see if they are there again. As you drive around, note the groups and the things that will help you identify them. Is it the same group hanging around on a regular basis? It may be that you recognise an item of clothing – a jacket or a baseball cap, for example. Try to assess who the leader is, and if there is a core group, with others who come and go, or if it's the same group each evening.

This can be frustrating as it takes time to recognise patterns, and these can change with seasons and holidays, so be aware of this as you are doing your surveillance. Also note when the clocks are about to go back or forward as this can have an effect.

You may be thinking that all this takes a long time. The local community profile will probably take about two months part-time, and the surveillance may take another two months. If it is not done and you start to meet young people, it may be that you meet a group as a one-off one week and never again and it is likely that you will run into problems later. The research gives you subjects to talk about – 'I hear there is a youth club, do you ever go?' – and it gets you known in the adult community. I would suggest that the project will become established more quickly through putting in the right foundations and using the time constructively, rather than pursuing a number of false starts. This does not mean that this method is foolproof though.

> The local community profile will probably take about two months part-time, and the surveillance may take another two months.

In Cheltenham we had identified a group of girls who hung around on the corner of one of the streets, on the edge of the estate. They were there every time we went out on surveillance, between about 5.30 to 7.30pm. We saw them for months, but didn't contact them, as we were two men. We saw them because we parked the car off the estate and walked past where they hung out. We recognised that we needed a female worker to target this group, but the week we found someone was the week the group disappeared. It was like the Bermuda triangle. A couple of years later, we were introduced to one of the girls from the group by the other young people, I asked her if she used to hang around on this street and it turned out she did and had remembered us walking past. I found out that the group hadn't split up as such, but something had come on the TV that they all wanted to watch. I think we had lost out to Neighbours, Dawson's Creek *or some other soap.*

Exploring the edges

● Draw an area around your home or where you work. Map it out from memory including the roads, phone boxes, shops, bus stops, information centres, shortcuts, schools, police stations, doctors etc.

● Read Acts 16:6–10. Why was Paul stopped by the Holy Spirit from going into Bithynia?

● Does this have any implications for the work you may do in a detached context?

● To what extent are you prepared to lay down your agenda and ideas of what you think God wants and be open to hear where he wants to take you?

Cold contact

5 Cold contact

Cold contact is traditionally seen as waltzing up to a group of complete strangers and introducing yourself as a youth worker. It has to be everyone's biggest fear about any kind of street work and this can sometimes produce surprising results.

> *A new worker started with us and was taken into the local school, where we operated a detached work project with young people on the edge of the school community. Completely new to the area and not knowing any young people, Steph decided to try to chat to two of the lads her co-worker had acknowledged earlier, and introduced herself. One of the lads replied, 'I'm S**tface and this is B*****d.' 'Fine.' said Steph and continued the conversation. It soon became clear that this off-the-cuff response of theirs was more of a joke than a challenge.*

In most cases this is a misconception. In my experience, this is the only incident of this kind. In reality, cold contact work is rarely confrontational. It does take time to build relationships, which is why in many cases cold contact becomes something of a myth.

Most people do not know what to say to young people when they first meet them on the streets. We must remember that the young person is just the same as any young person we have met. We should not be sucked into the negative media image of young people, or the local gossip, as it is very unlikely to be true.

Detached work is a long-term project and, as such, you do not have to walk up with a carefully prepared and rehearsed statement. You don't have to worry about the eternal significance for you and your projects' credibility just because you blow it and get your words muddled. The likelihood of saying 'Hi I'm working for Richard's wise youth subject' instead of saying 'Hi my name's Richard, I'm a detached youth worker for the Streetwise youth project' is minimal. Being a little nervous can be helpful, as you make sure you remember everything and are more dependent on God. I sometimes wonder if nerves are God's way of getting us to pay more attention to the Holy Spirit in difficult situations.

A starting point for cold contact is to think about how young people make friends, and then mirror the way they build relationships as you start your detached work. I remember I had to change schools when I was twelve. I was due to enter the second year (year 8) that September. The trouble was that everyone else had been there a year already, and many had come up from primary school together. As I didn't know anyone, I was dreading it. On the first day I was assigned a fellow student to show me around. Things didn't go too badly, I had a good sense of direction and wasn't getting lost all the time, but making friends took time. Looking back, I never went up to anyone out of the blue and introduced myself. You just don't do that as a young person. I would get talking to people and over a period of time, get invited by them to go down to town for lunch, or to play football.

Talking to young people nowadays, nothing much has changed. It still takes young people time to build relationships. I would describe any initial contact as usually being a brief acknowledgement that you exist, more of an 'Alright?' rather than a 'How are you?' The great thing about mirroring this approach is it also takes all the pressure off the introduction stage.

Cold contact should be more like a process of small unthreatening taps, rather than a big hit. Once you have identified the group or groups you hope to work with, initial contacts can be made. There are lots of ways of doing this, but the golden rule of detached work is 'don't try to contact someone on the move unless you know them'. The first stage is a level of acknowledgement. If the group hang around near a shop, go past them and buy something, and come back past them. Chip shops are great for this. This isn't about being covert, but mirroring the way relationships are built. The next time you go past the group acknowledge them by nodding your head. The next time say 'Alright?'. After a time of doing this it is then easy to initiate contact in a far more relaxed way. If the group meet in the park go and kick a ball around, and again acknowledge them before initiating further contact.

Hopefully, after the acknowledgement stage you should be feeling more relaxed about being on the young people's 'turf' and more able to initiate an introduction. I normally say something like 'Hi my name's Richard I've seen you around, I'm a detached youth worker.' At this point someone in the group usually says 'A what?' I explain, 'I'm a bit like a youth worker at the youth centre, but I meet young people on the streets, and as it's cold, next time you see us come over for a chat so I don't get bored'. This approach shows the young people that you value them, you know the estate has a centre, although you are not the same as the workers there (hopefully this way they don't stereotype you). It also shows you are aware they are often around and you have taken notice of them before and you will be around regularly. As it is fairly open ended the young people will often continue the conversation, but if the reception is chillier it gives you a chance to leave with a 'See you again', where they know you will contact them rather than wait for them to contact you. That's all there is to it. From there on you can build the relationship slowly, work out where God seems to be working and try to get in on the act. It may take more time with certain groups than with others, and it may seem to have taken a long time just to get to this point.

> 'I'm a bit like a youth worker at the youth centre, but I meet young people on the streets, and as it's cold, next time you see us come over for a chat so I don't get bored.'

A friend once suggested to me that one of the reasons Jesus was able to communicate so powerfully and build such deep relationships was that before he began his public ministry he had spent thirty years immersed in his culture. Many theologians suggest that the majority of the disciples were in their teens, much younger than Jesus. If this is the case, and you were considered a man far younger in that society than in today's, it begs the question, 'Why did Jesus wait so long to begin his public ministry?' Was he learning how to communicate and doing the groundwork as my friend suggested?

A big question within a relational style of youth work is when to say that you are a Christian? Is it important to say it from the outset? There are different schools of thought on the subject. Many people feel it is important to say it from the outset, others feel it creates a barrier, whilst others feel you may never need to say it. The example I gave of an opening statement in detached work didn't mention Christianity, but sometimes I would say I was a Christian detached youth worker, or a detached worker for Youth for Christ. At other times I wouldn't mention Christianity. However you approach the issue, Jesus clearly taught that deeds were more important than words. In terms of verbalising it, the important factor is to be authentic to the gospel and true to yourself. If in other areas of your life you naturally say to people early on that you are a Christian, and you feel comfortable with this, do it. If you don't, that's OK. If we are to live authentic gospel lives, the verbalisation and challenge of the gospel will come up at some point. My opening statements have just evolved and I say different things at different times. Whilst I wouldn't deny I was Christian, there have been times when I felt strongly I shouldn't say anything about Christianity when I introduced myself, and vice versa. Go with what feels comfortable, and examine your motives for saying you are a Christian. Do you feel pressure to say you are a Christian because you think your church expects it, or are you forcing yourself because of a fear of failure or a wrong view of God's requirements of you?

There are all kinds of ways of moving the work on after the acknowledgement stage other than a straightforward introduction. Initiating contact verbally, you could use the situation or context, ranging from the weather to boredom. It may be that you show your ID card and refer to the picture that makes you look like a convict. It could be that you refer to the young person, in some way, or look for common ground, eg 'I have a cap like that' (which hopefully they don't find insulting!). It is possible to use questions, though care needs to be taken that they are not threatening. Voicing an opinion or referring to a recent incident can be a good start point, but it is important to establish who you are quickly.

We decided to throw the frisbee around and see what happened. After a while the lads we had seen through our surveillance turned up. There were only two of them and they were kicking a tennis ball around. Phil and I carried on but we had both registered their arrival. They were standing behind Phil, so I threw the frisbee in their direction over Phil's head. As Phil picked it up he said 'Hi'. As we continued to play, I could see they were watching us, though Phil couldn't as they were behind him. I threw it short and as Phil came closer to pick it up I said they were watching us and I would throw towards the young people again so he could ask them to join us. This he did, after mentioning something about the size of their football, and as they joined in we explained who we were and what we were doing. It was easy to initiate conversation and after a while we were throwing the tennis ball around as well. It was a good, laid back start to detached work. They were about twelve at the time, and we kept contact with them the whole time we worked on the estate. These young people were proud that they were the first people we talked to, and would often mention that first game of frisbee, even five years on.

On top of the verbal starters mentioned earlier there are several other ways of making contact with young people. Again these work best after the acknowledgement stage. These, like the frisbee game, are there to start you off. It is still important that you explain who you are and what you are doing, particularly the first time you speak to a group. Equipment really helps you as you start to build on the initial contact. The week after we had played frisbee it was too windy to use the frisbee so we took a football out, and this built on the contact made the previous week.

There are a variety of games and sports equipment that can be used. Kites work well as many young people rarely use them, or footballs and basketballs. You don't have to have goals or baskets or even much space. We would challenge young people to hit the football in order from head, shoulders, knees and toes, knees and toes. There aren't many basketball nets, so we developed a street version. Instead of nets we would use two drain covers, standard basketball rules applied, (except no one knew them) and to score you had to bounce the ball on the drain. It worked best with metal covers as you could hear when someone scored as there was a different sound.

In some areas detached workers use shopping trolleys with a gas stove attached, and they make tea and hot chocolate. Videos and cameras can be used. Young people, like most adults will often try to avoid being photographed if they think they are just in the way. If you explain who you are and ask them to get in the picture it is often a great starting point. However, Child Protection procedures need to be adhered to when taking photographs and videos.

Animals and children can work well. If you introduce your baby to the young people, they are usually far more animated than you would expect young people to be. Walking a dog, you soon get to see the same young people regularly. Some projects use contact cards, and give them to the young people as contact is made, others such as health promotion detached projects may give out condoms as an icebreaker to explain the purpose of their project.

In the early days it is important to leave the impetus with the young person or group. When things are going well, the last thing you may feel like doing is leaving a good contact, but in the long term it may be better to choose to leave. Relationships are not built in a day, but take time. If you choose to leave, you can explain that you will be back next week and arrange to meet again and pick up where you left off. Also, it's better to leave on a high and not be the last one to leave.

> There will be times when you feel like a spare part. There may be times when you need to stick it out, just to be accepted for being there, they will draw you into conversation on their terms.

There will be times when you feel like a spare part. There may be times when you need to stick it out, just to be accepted for being there – they will draw you into conversation on their terms.

A brilliant example of detached work that sums up many of these principles (although I don't think Jesus played basketball!) is where Jesus speaks to the woman from Samaria in John 4. We see Jesus going on to her turf. He did the unexpected, he broke through cultural norms which should have kept them apart and he started where she was at. He was natural, he asked her to do something for him, put himself in her debt, built confidence and respect, and he relaxed her.

Exploring the edges

- You approach and engage a group that are sitting on a wall. They briefly acknowledge you, but make no effort to communicate, what do you do?

- Once you have passed the acknowledgement stage what could you say to young people?

- Look at John 4 as an example of detached work. What do you notice?

- What skills and talents do you have that may be useful to use as a non-verbal contact starter, eg sports?

- When is it relevant and authentic for you to say you are a Christian on the streets?

Re-learning old skills

6 Re-learning old skills

Discipline

The young people were always fascinated by our cars. Cars held a powerful mystique, as the young people's access to them was limited. Lots of the young people we knew were into 'twoccing' (taking without the owner's consent), and many times, when we hadn't seen a young person around, we later found out they had been banged up for exactly that. In the early days of detached work we would drive down to the areas we were working and park off the estate. Then as the relationships built, we would bring the car closer to the patches of work. It soon became apparent that this was a problem, as we had to get out of the car before the young people got in. When it was time to leave, a few of the young people would try to jump in or hang on the back. This was mainly good-natured, but there were times when a young person would refuse to get out. Trying to get a young person out of the car who didn't want to presented an interesting scenario. We could have physically removed young people from the car but that isn't very acceptable. Many of the young people we worked with had a tough time at home, often suffering from physical punishment or abuse. We could give the young person a lift, but that would set a precedent that others would never let us forget, and contravene good youth work practice. If we tried sanctions, like saying they couldn't come on the next trip, it often meant little and was repeating a cycle that the young person had experienced before. Often in the end it came down to a mixture of techniques ranging from ignoring them for a while, asking politely, asking again, explaining we had to go now, drawing on the

relationship we had built up and encouraging their friends to ask them
to get out. A lot of this was done whist thinking on our feet, always main-
taining a positive nature and trying never to show our frustration.

Often the way you approach situations on the streets is different from in a youth club or church setting. You are working with different young people, and the power base is vastly altered. Many of the traditional or more rational ways of approaching situations are different. Reasoning with young people who have little bargaining power is difficult. So many of the young people I used to work with had very few opportunities for trying new activities. Even though there were some good things to do in Cheltenham and the surrounding area, many young people had never taken part. Bowling was one activity that came to Cheltenham while we were there, but many of the young people on the estate never went of their own accord. Although there wasn't much money around, the young people weren't restricted from going by finance or the distance. When they had money it never occurred to them to go bowling, but if we suggested it, it was a good idea. After going they wanted to do it again, but wouldn't go by themselves.

In my mind this equated to a powerful bargaining tool – ideal when a young person was glued to the back seat of the car. But, in a conflict situation, it deemed to make no difference to them whether they went bowling or not. The young people never reasoned in this way. It was a bizarre paradox. There are many reasons for this and they are different for the individual young people concerned. For some, it was that things were often offered with one hand and taken away with another, or never materialised at all. Others didn't know what they would be missing, or it was just another one in a long line of missed opportunities. Reasoning itself wasn't something they were used to. Often the only way to approach a situation was to deal with it in the most adult way possible, but at times we had to be hard and very straight down the line. A useful tip is to use a clip-on mirror, designed for parents with toddlers in the back, when driving with young people. It allows you to keep an occasional eye out safely, and doesn't solely rely on having other workers present.

It is always important to treat the young people with respect, and love them even when dealing with difficult situations. The young people know that you respect and value them, and often this is important to them. They may also be aware that you treat them differently to the way other adults may. Using this in reasoning is possible but care needs to be taken, and consistency is essential. We would challenge them on the basis that they were adults and not children and so should behave like adults. In doing this it was vital not to talk down to them. If we spoke on an adult-to-adult basis it tended to lift their behaviour to an adult level. This seems a very basic approach, but works as the young people know that you respect them as adults by the way you have dealt with them in the past.

Life is different on the street, whether you live there or are just visiting. The boundaries and rules that are set in youth clubs are of little relevance. Could you imagine knocking on someone's front door, walking straight in and asking him or her not to swear as you talked about the day you have both had? If the streets are where young people feel at home, what is the difference? In youth clubs you set rules and ban people if they don't adhere to them. You can't bar someone from the park if they are smoking pot or cigarettes. You can challenge them but that is as far as it can realistically go.

> You can't bar someone from the park if they are smoking pot or cigarettes. You can challenge them but that is as far as it can realistically go.

I can never remember asking a young person in the first few years to watch their language. The young people began to modify their language themselves after a while, and then when on a trip or activity together, if it was noticeably different, another young person or I would point out unacceptable language. We may have sounded like a bunch of hooligans compared to your average Sunday youth group, but I noticed the change.

It may be the case that the young people you work with do not attend school. In this case there may also be different behaviour patterns that cannot be approached in traditional ways. It would be wrong to expect young people, who may have never known the structure of school or a formal youth work setting, to behave in the same way as those who do. That is not to say that standards should not be upheld, but that those standards must be defined and impossible expectations should not be made. Expecting the impossible causes hassle for all those concerned, both young people and workers. Change happens over time and is often best assimilated rather than forced.

Communication

Up to seventy percent of all communication is visual. We communicate through many ways including the way we listen and our body language.

Listening

The vital skill for all youth workers is listening. Young people desire to be listened to. It is an important part of growing up, helping the young person make the transition from child to adult as their views are heard and they vocalise them for themselves and begin to hear what is going on inside them. Often, young people will express views they have not thought through for themselves which are copied from their parents or culture around them. As they vocalise these views they realise that they are not what they truly think. I feel that listening to young people is an important way to break the cycle of negative attitudes and behaviour patterns. Listening is a powerful tool in itself but, when coupled with informal education, real change becomes possible. The two key words within listening are observation and communication. Without understanding the principles of communication within a given context we will not build relationships, and without observation, we will only hear what we want to hear. So often we speak before we have listened and we seek to affect, or communicate, into a culture before we understand it.

To really listen to people means that we have to examine our own preconceptions, and listen to ourselves. If we don't do this we may impose Christian culture on to these people and not present to them the naked gospel. We need to realise that we can learn from them about God and be open to hear what he is saying to us, through them. I have learnt a lot about what it means to be committed to one another from young people on the streets.

We also listen by not talking. Many young people will talk over one another and often this is part of their culture. We need to learn to follow the various conversations and ask for clarification when needed, without the other young people feeling unheard. When talking to individual young people on the street it is important not to interrupt. Young people will often struggle to communicate difficult feelings and search for words. There can be a tremendous desire to finish off sentences or volunteer words. With the often unforeseen nature of detached work this can be unhelpful as if you get it wrong it can make a young person, who is struggling to communicate, lose their flow. Summarising can be helpful, but again, as the young people are not often listened to, it can be wrongly viewed by the young person as an attempt to finish the conversation, or undermine their confidence as you put into a few phrases what took them five minutes to say.

Eye Contact

The eyes are the windows of the soul, you can see so much in a person's eyes. We can know if a person is close to crying long before they start, if we are watching their eyes. For many marginalised young people making eye contact can be disconcerting and even threatening. It is important, however, because it lets an individual know that they have your full attention and you are listening to them.

Facial expression

It is important that we are aware of the help and hindrance our facial expressions can be. If we go as red as a beetroot as a young person tells us of their sexual exploits what does that convey? If we gasp in horror as a young person explains what happened last night, are they likely to open up again? We also need to be aware of the young person's facial expression and what this tells us.

Bodily posture and common gestures

When we are taller than young people it can seem we are talking down to them emotionally as well as physically. We also need to be aware of the differing styles of body language that may exist on the street. What may be deemed as traditionally closed body language may simply be part of street culture and not mean anything at all. Beware of the change that happens when more people are added to the group, and the different culture of listening that may exist on the street. It is also helpful to be aware of your own body language, to convey that you are listening, and observing others, to hear what is behind their words.

Physical proximity

Physical proximity can be divided between social and intimate. For the majority of your work on the streets, social proximity should be maintained. There are times however when you may need to move closer to a young person who is opening up to you. By moving yourself around or to the side, you can draw the young person to the side of a group, where they may feel more confident to talk. It is important not to cramp a person's personal space. We have probably all experienced people who talk only inches from your face. On the streets there is so much space that you also need to be aware that sometimes the distance between individuals in a group is too great. If young people are used to the open space then they will naturally adjust to this greater space. It can feel intimidating at first to have a conversation with a group of young people sitting on a six-foot wall, or on top of a couple of telephone boxes. They will not feel inhibited and may have decided that it's a good place to watch the world go by.

> To even contemplate Christianity, may mean the young person feels they are rejecting their parents, family and peer group, turning their back on the society they know.

Appearance

Whether we like it or not we are judged on our dress sense. Young people are fashion conscious. This does not mean that we need to keep up with latest fashions but we do need to be aware of what we are wearing. I remember going to a big Christian meeting with a friend who introduced me to a game called 'Spot the denomination'. Long before hands went in the air he could tell an evangelical by their jumper or an evangelical minister because he had a jumper with a tie underneath. This is a rather tongue in cheek view of the church's dress sense, but the point is made. What message do we send out by what we wear, and is this a help or a hindrance?

We need to learn to communicate differently. On the streets it is vital that the right to speak is earned. It comes through being consistent, being around, following through on things, treating the young people with respect and compassion. This means you start being viewed in the light of who you are, rather than in the light of negative Christian stereotypes. The needs of young people need to be met. Communication needs to happen within a context of trust, security, significance and acceptance of the individual.

If you are working with pre-non-Christian young people then the gospel that you are conveying is alien to their culture. To even contemplate Christianity, may mean the young person feels they are rejecting their parents, family and peer group, turning their back on the society they know. The gospel needs to be lived within the culture you are working in. We need to show through our own lives that it is not about turning your back on your community and retreating to a cosy subculture called church. Rather, it is about a radical personal transformation over time, of individuals and communities.

Over five hundred years ago the printing press revolutionised the world through its ability to communicate information quickly and in bulk. Before this point, information was communicated through painstaking writing and copying articles and before this, information was passed on orally to the next generation. This is exactly how the gospels were communicated. Today, in our age of technology, we find ourselves orientated and bombarded by visual stimulation. The process and speed of communication and access to information through the computer age has made our world very small. The postmodern age that is emerging has asked many questions of the rational approach to education and communication. With a TV-orientated society, the way we think and hear and how we learn, has changed. In a world where the most powerful communications are visual, we have to reassess our communication techniques. The heart of communication is not words, but understanding and this is a two way process. Effective communication moves freely in both directions, building on feedback, it implies being understood and understanding. Living the gospel has become of vital importance – the medium is the message.

Stories can help us learn, initially as the hearer identifies with them, perhaps with a particular character, but later through remembering and reflecting on it. Jesus used stories that were interesting, easy to understand, and that held the attention. They demanded a response, and were relevant to the situations of the people who heard them. Many young people's only encounter with the church, and therefore with Jesus, has been through the media's portrayal, which is often distorted. You will need to deconstruct any misconceptions that have little reference to the radical Jesus, we know and reconstruct them, giving them more correct information and allowing them to make their own minds up. Drawing on your own story is also vital, it shows a transparency that is counter to the culture of which they are part. Many of the young people will be without basic knowledge of the Bible narrative, the cycle of the perfect creation, man messing it up, God stepping in again and again as man fails and Jesus being the ultimate way that God steps in. Retelling Bible stories in ways they can relate to, drawn in at appropriate times, helps to build a framework to help the young person see in a different way.

'[The Son] can do only what he sees his Father doing, because whatever the Father does the Son also does.' (John 5:19) To watch and see what the Father is already doing, in communities others have labelled as dark or godless, takes time. We need to learn to listen to the heartbeat of the street as we go about our work. There will be times when we can tell something is different, or extra care is needed and other times when we really sense something is changing.

> When the weather started getting better I would walk to our office which was about twenty minutes off the estate. In the evenings on the way home I would often see young people I knew, stop and chat or say 'Hi' as they cycled past. Throughout the winter there had been young people around who we saw regularly, but now the weather was getting better we started to build up some more contacts. It had been a difficult few weeks and two of the young people I knew well had been sent to prison. As I trudged home, I noticed a small yellow flower had pushed up through the pavement, about a foot from the nearest garden. It was astounding that this creation, not much bigger than a buttercup, had been able to force its way through the layers of stone and tarmac. I wondered if its beauty came like the new butterfly struggling to get out the cocoon: that the struggle made the blood fill the wings and that was where the beauty stemmed. I also knew that the flower wouldn't last long on the pavement and was tempted to pick it and preserve it, but I knew it would only be a shadow of its former self out of the environment it was in. I held onto the image as a symbol of hope in difficult times and when out on detached work the following evening explained what I had seen to some of the young people. I sensed it gave them hope as well, and my hope was that this was real, not a wishful imagination.

Exploring the edges

● Ask a friend to help you explain your day to them, maintaining good eye contact. Then ask them to explain their day whilst you listen to them without talking. Get your friend to comment on how well they think you listen both generally and in this exercise.

● What is your story and how much personal detail are you willing to share with young people?

● Retell a parable changing the characters and situation but still maintaining the main point.

● What are the major misconceptions a young person may have about Christianity and how would you explain them?

● Examine how you normally talk to young people. Is it on an adult to adult basis? If not, why not?

7 Change not control

Change

Nipper could be a nightmare. We knew his older brother well, but Nipper had only recently started hanging around with the group. Whatever was going on, he was into it. He had been in and out of trouble with the police most of his life, and had also been taken into care on and off. Now he was around more he had started to join in with some of the things we did on the streets. Nipper had been excluded from school and often got into trouble because he was bored. He wanted to come on trips with us, but was almost uncontrollable. One of the aims in our work was not to be a provider of activities but to facilitate the young people to plan their own activities and learn through the process. Nipper didn't lack confidence; he was bright and intelligent, but all the children in the family had had a pretty rough time growing up, some going to prison and a couple of his older brothers were not able to read or write. He was aware that unless he took part in planning the activities we weren't going anywhere, however he really wanted to try kite flying. At the beginning we were well aware that he wasn't going to have the necessary skills to plan much, so we started by asking him to get together with three other people and work out when they wanted to go kite flying. When we saw him next he said that he had arranged it for the following afternoon. We arranged to pick him up, but when we arrived there was only Nipper there. In the end we went and had a great time. As we drove back from the hills we asked Nipper what he thought of kite flying. He replied 'It's better than nicking cars!'

That was the beginning of a change for Nipper. We slowly increased his responsibility in the planning of trips and activities and he learnt a lot through the process. The process of supporting a young person to undertake responsibilities is called scaffolding. Whether we like it or not, we are role models to young people. Youth work is educational. Young people will pick things up from us, good and bad, and will learn. With this in mind, it is important within the context of our youth work, to help young people mature into adults and teach them the skills they will need to function in society.

Youth workers often make the assumption that they seek to bring about social change in the lives of young people: change in lifestyle, change in attitude, spiritual change, educational change. Sometimes this is not achieved and it becomes about the young person becoming socially acceptable, changing behaviour patterns, taking their place in society and becoming like us, rather than enabling the young person to challenge the status quo, to resist the temptation to be one of the many. The former is social control of young people rather than social change. Social control isn't simply about power to rule or act over young people. Social control involves the active promotion of ideas and values which aim to reinforce the status quo. Everything from the media to the police is engaged in this activity. If we are to be effectively facilitating change then we need to ask what kinds of change we are promoting. As Christians, serving young people should be a key principle of our youth work. If we explore what it truly means to serve others, it causes us to ask serious questions of our youth work and ourselves. To serve means denying ourselves, not putting our values, notions, ideas or self before those we seek to serve. The implications of this kind of service are huge. It leads us full circle, not maintaining social control in any way, but becoming agents of change that seek out new places to travel with young people on their spiritual journey.

> **serving young people should be a key principle of our youth work.**

As Vincent Donovan says,

> *In working with young people, do not try to call them back to where they were, and do not try to call them to where you are, as beautiful as that place may seem to you. You must have the courage to go with them to a place that neither you nor they have ever been before.* [11]

Jesus taught that change comes through giving up ourselves. He demonstrated it by giving up his life so that we have the opportunity to change. By linking Donovan's words with the key principle of youth work – empowerment, equal opportunities, informal education and participation – we begin to create a curriculum framework for good detached work. A work where we relinquish ourselves, go to the people, build real, equal relationships and continue that process wherever it leads. If we accept this challenge in our youth work, I believe we will see a radical shift, which will enable us to deliver the true message to the masses rather than to the few.

Informal education

It was so hot! This was detached work at its best. The sun was blazing, there wasn't a cloud in the sky, and it was mellow, in more than one sense of the word. The young people were relaxed and chilled. It was too hot to play football, so we just sat on the grass chatted, and occasionally someone would pop down to the shop for more cold drinks or ice pops. Speculation was rife amongst the young people, as to where Shearer would end up next season, and to start with, football was the main topic of conversation. We were lounging in the park near the adult learning centre, and as the conversation meandered along someone asked, 'Why is this place on our estate'. I asked him what he meant, and we ended up in a group discussion on disability, which wasn't hostile but continued to meander in the way it had all day. Soon the conversation had twisted and turned and we had covered related subjects such as racism, immigration and sexism, as well as others like the law, Christianity, the Gulf War and most other subjects under the sun. We chatted for hours and different attitudes were explored and challenged, both theirs and mine. They would challenge each other, drawing on real life examples and questioning what they would do if they were in a certain situation. Whilst I occasionally challenged a comment, I more often stated some facts which were then chewed over by the group. The conversation became really heated, but it was also clear that views were changed. By the time we got home we were sunburnt and tired, but amazed at the depth of what had happened during those hours in the sun.

We all learn in different ways, but probably the most important education for most of us was received informally, when we were unaware that we were being educated. We learn things throughout our lives by watching others. Many things are learnt in the first six years of life and for the majority of that time there is no formal education. Informal education is taking place all the time. However, if we work with this, informal education can become a powerful tool in youth work. Detached work is an effective setting for informal education because of its informality.

Certain characteristics of informal education need to be kept in mind when engaging young people in the process. Learning can be incidental or unplanned but is always purposeful and deliberate. Anything can start off a conversation but the direction it takes can be steered or directed. As it is informal it is not time-structured and it is not about making a point. The learners are voluntary participants and so control is minimal. A young person can get up and walk away at any time. To be effective it must involve dialogue based on mutual respect and two-way communication. In my years working with young people I have learnt so much from them, like friendship and gratitude. I am constantly challenged to think about my views, and examine why I hold them. In informal education you approach as learners together. It is experiential and involves direct participation in the events of life.

Tools such as board games can help the process, and these often use role-play to ground the learning into reality. As a detached worker you can use the things around you to do this. I would often find we were exploring a topic that had arisen in the news or happened to someone on the estate. Or I would open up a conversation using what was around us. I remember sitting with a lad who was feeling down. He felt stuck in his job and was unsure where his future was heading. As we were sitting on a roundabout, I asked if he ever felt that his life was going round in circles. This was the opening he needed to talk and we explored ways he could move forward.

Informal education works alongside existing social, economic, and political situations. It often provides a starting point that is continued in a more formal setting. As already stated, informal education is a purposeful process, and as such we can identify seven different stages in the process. Using these we are able to formulate our thoughts and they provide a loose structure that helps us, as workers, serve young people more fully.

Self awareness

The educator needs to be aware of their own strengths, weaknesses and attitudes. Where you may have differing or negative attitudes these need to be thought through. It is helpful to be aware of our own short-comings.

Relationship

There needs to be some sort of relationship between educator and learner based on mutual respect.

Listening

The educator needs to listen for appropriate areas to educate, listening to the person, the situation and context in order to be able to challenge appropriately.

Challenge

There needs to be an understanding of how to challenge or question in an appropriate and effective manner.

Exploration

Explore, sensitively, the thoughts and feelings of the group about the subject or related issues. As in the discussion in the park, the conversation must be allowed to flow from subject to subject, but the conversation must be grounded in people's experience thus enabling the young people to open up more of themselves.

Disengage

The educator needs to recognise when and how to disengage a conversation. Often it is better to finish a conversation earlier rather than later. We need to be aware that some subjects may bring up painful memories for individuals and it may not be appropriate to discuss these with the whole group.

Continuance

The educator may find that the group wishes to pursue a subject in more detail, for example, drug awareness. Who will take action? More information can be researched or external help brought in.

Informal education is an effective way of challenging young people with the gospel. It is well suited to use with pre-non-Christians, and works well within the existing youth culture and post modern climate.

Challenge is a key element in any form of youth work. Challenging appropriately varies depending on the context, and is very hard to write about as so many factors come into play. Every group of young people is different, as is every individual and every situation. You may meet the same group every day, but each day they will have had a different experience that may mean the challenge has to be framed differently or not given at all. It may be that you only find out it wasn't a good time to challenge a statement after you have done so. To challenge is to risk, but without taking risks there would be no effective detached work.

How and when do we challenge young people? There are numerous opportunities to challenge, but it will not be appropriate to take them all. A good starting point could be when a young person tells a joke at the expense of others, the worker can challenge their attitudes and behaviour. It is important to challenge the idea not the person, and to do so sensitively, with open-ended statements or questions, thus giving opportunities for the young person to respond. For example, 'I haven't heard you express that opinion before' or 'Why do you say that?' rather than 'You can't say that'. Once an initial comment is made, it is important to give the space for the young person to reply, and this gives you the chance to gauge whether it was a good time to initiate informal education or not. It may well be that after the first challenge you need to offer another question to show you are willing to chat and encourage the young person to respond.

All of us are on a journey. Young people are on a journey of discovery and adventure. They are pushing back boundaries and checking out frontiers. When exploring, it is best to have a guide who can help point out the odd thing missed, but not a guide who controls the pace. The use of informal education in detached work is similar to the concept of mentoring, which has an important role in detached work. I find mentoring a more helpful term than 'discipling' as mentoring majors on relationships and is young person initiated, whereas discipling focuses on discipline, and tends to be leadership driven. Mentoring is not counselling, rather it is walking beside. It costs prayer, time and energy.

Jesus used informal educational methods to train his disciples, often through telling stories. He gave on the job training, allowing for mistakes, getting frustrated and having another go. The learning was organic and grounded in real life situations. He encouraged by living, walking and being with his disciples. He used day to day situations to learn, he asked questions, used shock and surprise and often told stories without explaining them. He left room for self discovery and ownership. He used all the senses; he painted pictures and communicated through the raw energy of the day. He used history and connected with people in a deep and powerful way.

> Mentoring is not counselling, rather it is walking beside. It costs prayer, time and energy.

Scaffolding

The way Jesus taught the disciples is similar to the concept of scaffolding. Scaffolding is about providing the right level of support to enable a young person to achieve a given task. It may be that much support is required and the worker only asks the young person to undertake a small part. As the process continues more responsibility can be passed on and the young person learns vital life skills throughout the various tasks undertaken. The aim being that no scaffolding is required in the end, as the young person becomes fully empowered.

Exploring the edges

Can we only challenge young people within the context of a relationship?

● What standards and principles do you adhere to that may impact your practice?

What should we do with verbal abuse, sexism, and racism?

What is an appropriate challenge?

What are the differences in challenging groups and individuals?

How do we share the gospel in an informal way?

How do we learn best?

To what extent does knowledge equate to power in the church? Should it?

Do we need to read to become a Christian?

Why are all our discipleship courses book-led? What are the advantages or disadvantages of systematic training courses that focus on knowledge rather than experience?

Development plans

8 Development plans

This chapter provides a framework for churches to develop strategies for establishing a project or to move a detached work project, or to further develop an existing project.

It is almost impossible to measure detached work, and harder still to assess change. If we are to truly seek change we must provide a framework for that change. If we aim at nothing, that is usually what we achieve. The development plan that follows (see overleaf) seeks to be such a framework that will facilitate positive unrestricted change. As we were working in a missionary context in Cheltenham, we worked according to a strategy based on my previous experiences of detached work, and refined it more formally only after some time in Cheltenham. It gave us some ways of measuring where we were going, but due to the nature of the work, it was really only a framework.

This development plan was used within a missionary context, as we were seeking to grow a culturally relevant church. I have therefore adapted it to be used in a variety of settings but it is only intended to provide a starting point and will need to be refined further to fit your circumstances.

Explanation of plan

Stages 1–3 Surveillance and cold contact (see earlier chapters)

Stage 4 – Area based work

This is when you are starting in an area and a wide variety of contacts are being made. Young people should be made fully aware of who you are and your role. You should begin to identify the interests of young people in the whole area.

Stage 5 – Peer group work

This happens as the work becomes more defined and natural groupings of young people are identified, often large and based around a shared interest. We used to meet a group of young people playing football which was mixed in sex and age and ranged in numbers from six to thirty with an average size of sixteen. This size group may not be present in your area. If not, the relationships can still be built in a similar way, preparing the ground for the next stage. The worker should be aiming to meet these groups informally twice a month, building a clearer picture of the young people's needs and interests. A trip roughly once a term could also be organised. The young people should also be aware that workers are available to them if they need them.

Stage 6 – Basic small group work

The work should be reaching this stage when you have identified the key 'leaders' in the group. An organised trip should happen around once a month and weekly contact should be made with these individuals. Any such group is likely to be made up from the young people that exist within the larger peer group. Based on the interests of the young people, you should look for hobbies within the group to develop fresh opportunities for such meetings.

Stage 7 – Risky small group work

This is about taking calculated risks to move the existing work and relationships forward positively. This can be done through one-to-one work, relaxing together or perhaps having a meal with the young people. If it has not happened already, the basics of the gospel could also be verbally shared. This is about opening up more of your lifestyle to the young

Detached work development plan

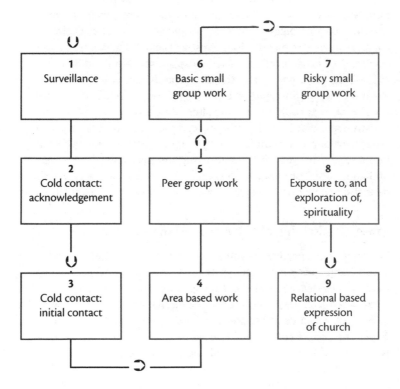

1 Surveillance	6 Basic small group work	7 Risky small group work
2 Cold contact: acknowledgement	5 Peer group work	8 Exposure to, and exploration of, spirituality
3 Cold contact: initial contact	4 Area based work	9 Relational based expression of church

people. It could be described as moving from being a youth worker to being a friend. This was also the stage where I was happy for young people to be in my home regularly. It is important you are confident with the young people before you do this, as once the door is open it is very difficult to shut.

Stage 9 – Exposure to, and exploration of, spirituality

Young people should be introduced to aspects of Christianity in practical, supportive ways. These can include events to raise their consciousness of bigger things, eg watching the sunrise, exploring creation or going to an organised Christian event. If you choose to take them to a Christian event you should explain some of the things that may happen beforehand, and translate what is happening during the event. Use the opportunity to explore spiritual issues in a supportive way. Events that could be used are alternative services, as well as local churches and youth groups. If a young person initiates conversation around making a decision for Christ, then you may invite such a decision, stressing that you will continue to support the individual regardless of their choice. You should also expect to have had some sort of residential experience with the group prior to this stage, or as part of it.

Stage 10 – Relational based expression of church

This refers to supporting the young people in local churches or relevant groups, and developing new groups where the young people can develop their own expression of a discipleship group with you.

Between each stage there are tools or mechanisms that enable work to progress onwards. These are varied and depend on the interests of the young people concerned. It could be kite flying, sports, hobbies, issues being discussed and explored, trips, or anything you do as group together that helps deepen relationships.

It is possible to identify the groups you are working with and 'guesstimate' where you are on the development plan. From there, decide where you wish the group to be in six months time and how you propose to get there. The plan will enable you to gauge your progress, provide a focus for prayer and generate a positive overview of the project to communicate to your supporters and church.

The following plan and graphs indicate a method by which targets can be set and progress can be monitored. Let us assume that we are working with seven groups of young people – labelled A–G. It is possible to determine where each group is on the plan and where you would like it to be in six months time. This can be plotted on a graph (shown on p84).

A mechanism should be devised to help reach the desired stage on the plan which, can be implemented during the six month period.

In six months time the process can be repeated and, over time, progress can be monitored and changes made as appropriate. By adopting this method, the story, development, successes and failures of the project can be all be evaluated.

Six month development plan

GROUP	CURRENT	DESIRED	MECHANISM
	STAGE 1 Jan	STAGE 1 Jun	
A	2	4	Initiate conversations and show ID, explain role.
B	5	6	Identify small group around age-groups, and take a trip together.
C	7	8	Take group on residential trip and do early morning sunrise walk to provoke discussion.
D	9	9	Use a contemporary 'soap' like *Eastenders*, *Neighbours* etc which portray vicars, clergy, church. Get group to express views on what church should be like.
E	3	5	Try to move group two stages to join with group G, by ensuring twice weekly contact.
F	6	7	Invite group to play video games and consolidate with two to three trips.
G	4	5	As group members are interested in football like group E, see if they know each other and arrange a match on a Saturday morning. Then look to take a trip out with the most open members of mixed group to establish new basic small group.

Detached groups 1st Jan

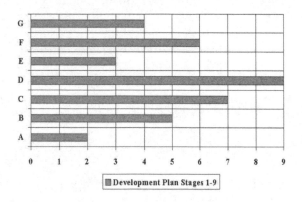

Development Plan Stages 1-9

Detached groups 1st June

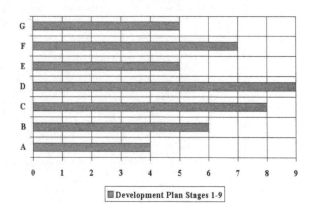

Development Plan Stages 1-9

Exploring the edges

- Where on the plan would you place any groups you are currently working with? Why?

- What activities have you used in the past with young people? How have these helped to develop relationships?

- How could this type of plan help you to communicate to others what you are trying to do in detached work?

- How does this plan fit with church-based youth work? Are there any crossovers?

- Is measuring what you are doing something that is important? Why? Or why not?

- Are the stages of development the same in your area? What you are trying to achieve, particularly in the last stage?

- How does this plan fit with the ethos and possible curriculum for youth work mentioned in the previous chapter?

Conflict, rejection and risk

9 Conflict, rejection and risk

While on my way home one evening, I heard shouting and screaming in the next street. As I turned the corner I couldn't believe it, the house was wrecked: the windows smashed, the door kicked in – fence torn down, drainpipes ripped off. It looked like there had been a hurricane. I knew the family who lived there and the oldest boy, Scott. Scott was as hard as they come, and was scary as he punched first, and rarely thought about the consequences. His mum had had a difficult time bringing up three boys on her own, and they were wild. Scott was the oldest at sixteen and had been expelled from school for fighting, and never tried to go to another; the younger two were eight and four.

I saw Jim further down the street, who I knew well, and asked him to tell me what had happened. He said that the youngest boy had been accused of trying to rape a neighbouring girl of the same age. Her older brother had discovered the little boy in the garden lifting up the girl's dress. The girl's extended family had jumped to action and run Scott's family off the estate. All this had happened the previous day and Scott was now riding around the estate with a baseball bat (which I think he stole from us) ready to batter any of the extended family he could find. The commotion earlier was because he had just gone past, taunting those in the street that knew him.

This situation was eventually concluded, but at the time it was the closest I have felt to walking into a lion's den. As Christians we find ourselves called to take risks. The first time we speak to our own families about our faith we risk rejection. As detached workers we are putting ourselves at risk: risking our actions being misinterpreted, risking violence, risking rejection and accusation. The poem below highlights some of the reasons why risk is important if we want to live authentic, transparent lives on the streets.

To laugh is to risk appearing the fool,
To weep is to risk appearing sentimental,
To reach out is to risk involvement,
To expose feelings is to risk exposing your true self,
To place your ideas and dreams before the crowd is to risk their love,
To love is to risk not being loved in return,
To live is to risk dying,
To hope is to risk despair,
To try is to risk failure,
But the greatest hazard in life is to risk nothing.
The one who risks nothing does nothing, and has nothing, and finally is nothing,
He may avoid suffering and sorrow,
But he simply cannot learn, feel, change, grow or love.
Chained by certitude, he is a slave, he has fortified freedom.
Only the one who risks is free!
Author unknown

In *Journey Towards Holiness*, Alan Kreidar likens Christians to either pioneers or settlers.[12] If we, as detached workers, are to journey to a new place with young people, we are pioneers, leaving what is known and moving forward together. As responsible adults often working with vulnerable young people, we need to expect the unexpected and be as prepared as possible for what lies ahead. Most of us will remember the lectures given by our school teachers before we went on trips: about how we were ambassadors for the school, that people would know who we were, and how, if we messed it up, we would spoil it for the next group. Trying to resist sounding like a teacher, most of the above is true. We must not take our responsibility lightly, but act responsibly and professionally preparing the ground for future workers. Some of the issues that need to be thought through are raised in the next chapter.

Protection

On the streets we find ourselves in many different and difficult situations, especially around the area of physical touch. Physical contact is an extremely difficult area to deal with. We know the importance of physical contact, but in an age when so much is misconstrued we need to find the balance of being beyond reproach, whilst trying to build authentic relationships with young people who are often in real need. So in this work we put ourselves at risk. Child Protection Policies must be adhered to. As a guide they provide valuable insights around the issues of physical contact. How do you comfort a hurt or crying young person? Would you put your arm around them? What if the reason they were crying was because an adult had abused them? If you are on the street, how is the situation going to be interpreted by passers by?

Physical contact is not the only area of risk. Use of the car can cause problems, especially if young people need a lift home. You may need to drop the last two off together so you are not left in a one-to-one situation. Then there are legal issues regarding insurance, public liability, etc.

> How do you comfort a hurt or crying young person? Would you put your arm around them? What if the reason they were crying was because an adult had abused them?

When you are planning a trip there are issues to do with consent forms, minibus drivers and insurance. There are many helpful resources on all these issues and they can be adapted to suit your project. There are also full time advisors, such as the denominational youth officers or those working with Christian organisations such as Frontier Youth Trust who can help with these issues. Another important point of contact is the local authority youth service who will have a worker responsible for the voluntary sector who should be able to offer help.

We cannot plan for every eventuality, but we can take steps to find out what issues we are likely to face and take steps to protect the young people and ourselves against them. Written records are an important part of this and are discussed in the next chapter.

Working in pairs or teams is also important in detached work. It seems to be a New Testament model: Jesus sent his disciples out in pairs, and even sent two to collect a donkey for his entry in to Jerusalem. In biblical terms it seems that two is the smallest conceiveable number of people. Where two or three are gathered, God is present (Matt 18:20). It is practical for safety and legal reasons, as you are witnesses to one

It is important to recognise the limitations of your role as this will help you reduce the risks you take.

another. It is also good to have someone to chat to on quiet nights, and you can be an encouragement for each other. When it was cold and wet there were times that my only motivation to go out on detached work was that I knew my co-worker was coming to collect me. Another important aspect is that it keeps young people from idolising you. Often your co-worker gets to know you well and can be more honest about your shortcomings than perhaps you are.

It is important to understand your role as a youth worker. You are not there in an authoritative way, as some sort of soft police officer. You are not there to control behaviour, neither are you there as a social worker. As a detached worker you support and facilitate the young people to achieve what is achievable, to broaden horizons and open eyes. It is important to recognise the limitations of your role as this will help you reduce the risks you take.

There are times that you will need to talk one-to-one with young people, but this can be done in the sight of your co-worker. There may also be times when you may feel you need to meet a young person to talk more, or go with them to a point of referral. Whilst ideally you should never be alone with a young person, if you need to meet one-to-one, use your common sense, and meet in a public place, eg at McDonalds, and always with a young person of the same gender. Furthermore, tell another adult that you are doing so, and refer to your organisation's Child Protection Policies.

All workers on the detached project must go through a selection process. This usually means filling in an application form and having an interview. (Your church should follow a similar procedure before allowing anyone to work with those under 18. If they do not, contact the Churches Child Protection Advisory Service, CCPAS, tel: 0845 120 455 or at: www.ccpas.co.uk – they can help your church to implement this.) If the worker is likely to have sole access to young people under 18, then it is highly recommended that they are checked by the Criminal Records Bureau at the enhanced level. (This will check for any police action which has not yet come to court.) The CRB form must be countersigned by a registered agency. Your church is unlikely to be registered but your denomination may be. Alternatively CCPAS will act as a registered body, on instruction from your church.

Rejection

Quin was the youngest of several. His family was notorious on the estate, and were recognised by both the police and the community as major perpetrators of crime. His older brothers stole, and did so with some success, although they were often in and out of prison. They also carried knives and were not to be messed with. By the time we had started work on the estate Quin was the only one who had not been to prison. We first got to know him when he was twelve. He was quite good at football, and he was slight in build and very fast. Over the years we built a slow but meaningful relationship. We often talked about his family situation and his desire to be different. I really thought we were getting somewhere but then I found out that he had been twoccing. I felt let down, and talked it through with him and we looked at some of the options for him. I didn't see Quin for while after that, and when we finally caught up he explained what he had been doing and was honest enough to include some of the illegal activities. When I challenged this, it was clear he had decided to part company from me and follow in his family's footsteps. I tried to explain that I would be there if he needed help at any time day or night and he knew where I lived. As he wandered away, I felt grieved and lost. I felt that four years had just gone down the drain, and the emotional pain became almost physical as I tried to pray. It took time to get over the incident. Through disciplined prayer, I was able to reach a point of faith that the years had not been spent in vain. It was vanity for me to think they had, because in doing so I had limited God, who is the God of the impossible. As I re-examined my call to the estate, I was aware of God's grace in my weakness, and his plan and purpose for the individuals as he filled the gap left in me by Quin's rejection.

Rejection is something we all have to cope with from time to time. In detached work we risk both ourselves and the message we carry being rejected. I remember Phil describing our work as being 'like standing on the top of a cliff trying to grab young people before they fall over the edge.' Often in detached work it can seem like this. Young people you know and care for get involved in situations that end up causing harm to them, either physically, emotionally or spiritually, and there is nothing you can do about it. Learning to reflect and take time out is an important tool. We should firstly assess who or what is being rejected and take steps to discover why. In looking at the issue of personal rejection the first question to ask is why you are doing the work? From here we need to view our motives and responses carefully. If we are motivated by a personal need, from guilt, or another motive other than God's calling, we will struggle when rejection comes.

Conflict can be healthy: we can transform this, and it is better than apathy. If a pre-non-Christian expresses a negative statement about God, this can be very positive, as God is now on their agenda. We have seen in earlier chapters how much is stacked against us in terms of culture, media and personal values. As we examine the rejections we encounter, we need to do so in the light of the above, rather than in the isolation of the incident. In doing this we can see new ways of meeting this rejection, and assess if it is appropriate to contact the young people further, challenging the cause of the rejection, rather than the symptom of the rejection itself. When any rejection occurs it is important to deal with it, openly seeking help from God and others, rather than letting any issues or conflicts build up.

Exploring the edges

- What are the advantages of working in pairs and threes?

- Examine and reflect on where your security lies – Is it on your ability, on God, or a combination of the two?

- You are working with a group of young people that are open to you; one girl starts to touch the male worker, what do you do?

- For the following questions, indicate what you would do by circling the appropriate number. '1' is for never and '5' is for always. Then discuss and analyse the answers with a friend. Answer with your gut reaction.

1 Would you ever kiss a young person?
1 2 3 4 5

2 Would you ever hug a young person?
1 2 3 4 5

3 Would you ever allow a young person to sit on you?
1 2 3 4 5

4 Would you physically comfort a hurt or crying young person?
1 2 3 4 5

5 Do you think it's a good idea to wrestle playfully with young people?
1 2 3 4 5

6 Would you allow a young person to kiss you?
1 2 3 4 5

7 Would you allow yourself to be alone with a young person?
1 2 3 4 5

8 Do you worry that a young person may touch you in a sexual way?
1 2 3 4 5

9 Would you hit a young person?
1 2 3 4 5

10 Would you stroke a young person's hair?
1 2 3 4 5

The big
Issues

10 The big issues

Harm reduction

We were playing football one evening, in what had been the church car park. Two old shopping trolleys served as goal posts at one end, with a traffic cone and a bike at the other. The ball was a bit flat, which was just as well as the site wasn't that big and there were about six of us playing. It had been a lively night so far: earlier, a five-year-old called Tank, a younger brother of one of our contacts, had beaten up a girl a couple of years older. Then her cousin had come to batter Tank. They were eventually pulled apart when I managed to persuade the older relations it was not a good idea to let the fight continue. The football was a welcome diversion, although as everyone was in high spirits, few rules were adhered to. That, however was nothing new for this part of the patch. Another group had formed just the other side of the fence and was obviously up to something. I couldn't tell what it was and I didn't know the young people in that group so well, but they seemed to be passing something around. Then one of the lads jumped over the fence and approached the goalkeeper with whatever it was they had been passing around earlier. I saw that it was a small aerosol can of some description. The group hadn't been sniffing it, but were just larking around. We had a chat about the issues and the dangers which was quite productive. It seemed that they weren't intent on trying any solvents but they would not give me the aerosol and I dared not try and persuade them for too long in case it became an issue. I explained my dilemma as a youth worker. My main concern was that they were safe, but I could not hang around and condone what they were doing . I explained the dangers. I then said I would go and see who else was around and would catch up with them later. Although I didn't expect them to try anything, I knew that this way I could come back in a couple of minutes to check they were OK.

We need to be aware that, when we are on the streets, things are not neatly packaged. It is raw, risky, messy and unpredictable. You meet different issues each time you go out. The young people's moods can swing, and their behaviour can be affected by the weather. Violence may be rare, but it often seems you are not that far away from a stand-off between two young people and it is always a plus when one backs down. One of the priorities of a detached worker is to ensure that the young people are safe, as all sorts of issues can arise and unexpected things can happen.

On one occasion, Phil was doing detached work in a local park and a young person climbed a rugby post. A while later they were chatting on the edge of the park when they saw the post start to lean, and the top fell down and hit a young boy on the head. Phil checked the lad out who was lying on the floor and one of the others went for help. Thankfully the lad was OK, but he was taken to hospital for a check up. This lad had nothing to do with Phil, but he was able to help.

'Harm reduction' is a method used to reduce the risks to young people of the various activities they may engage in. It is primarily education based and helps people to become aware of dangers. It is used within drug education as a way to reduce the risks of drug taking. It is often wrongly thought to be promoting drug use, as it promotes safer drug use and encourages people to use less harmful drugs or combinations of drugs. Harm reduction is often used in cases where workers do not see abstinence as an achievable goal, but would rather help users draw the line at soft drug use.

Harm reduction relating to substance misuse could be defined in the following way: [13] Harm reduction is an approach to education, which aims to reduce the harm from drug use. It does this by *providing accurate and correct information about drug use and its risks:*

● developing the skills for safer drug use.

- promoting more accepting attitudes towards drug users.

- encouraging existing and would-be drug users to discover safer ways of using and thus reducing the harm of drug use.

A harm reduction ladder is a method used to gauge the harm caused by using particular drugs or combinations of drugs. The higher the rung on the ladder, the higher the risk to the user. For example, someone injecting would be high up the ladder, followed by a poly-user (someone using a combination of drugs), a regular amphetamine/ecstasy user would be lower, then towards the bottom rung a weekend alcohol user, with a weekend cannabis user below this. Harm reduction is a recognised approach and is accepted by many professionals as a positive step forward in drugs education. There is a lot of evidence of its effectiveness helping substance abusers.

> 'Harm reduction' is accepted as a positive step forward in drugs education.

Matt had been a prime contact. I had known him for several years and it was strange now that he was working. We had done a lot together, planned a trip to a theme park, raised money for a camp, and talked about a lot of family issues. We had often talked about his family events as they seemed quite a laugh. Matt had a large extended family and always had some funny story to relate. I wish I could tell stories like he could. Someone would have fallen off the table whilst dancing, or collapsed in heap. His dad even fell asleep in the wardrobe one night. Alcohol was always part of the stories, and usually the reason why something had happened. Now Matt was older and off doing his own thing, I would hear the stories of what he had been up to on the previous weekend. At sixteen he was working, and he was drinking both with his mates from work, and with friends who I knew through detached work. Although he could tell a great story and joke, he wasn't overly popular, but he would always end up doing something memorable when he got drunk. He had fallen through a window, ripped a tent in two, and now as we chatted, his hand was bandaged, as he had got into a fight at a nightclub. It would take a long time to bring Matt to a realisation that whilst he wasn't an alcoholic, getting drunk wasn't doing him any good. We explored areas of self-esteem and he agreed to try not to get so drunk and to accept responsibility for his actions.

The question we must ask ourselves relating to harm reduction, as with many of the other issues encountered on the street, centres around our role as a detached worker. Should we accept, transform, or live with the tension between these two approaches? Are we:

a) condoning their behaviour?

b) conforming to their culture?

c) challenging their situation?

I believe that we need to take people from where they are, not from where we would like them to be. One of the inconsistencies of the church is that while we say that the most important thing is for people to change on the inside, we often look for outward evidence first, and rarely give people a chance or the time to change within. When Jesus met people in his own culture he spoke to them in a positive, not negative, way. 'Go now and leave your life of sin' (John 8:11). In his letter to the Colossians (2:20–23) Paul urges that it is pointless to tell a person not to do something, as people need to come to that decision themselves. We need to be aware that the young people we are in contact with, in detached settings, have no idea of what conversion is, in contrast to those who have been brought up in a Christian environment. Living in a post-Christian society, we are left with generations of people with no roots, who are unwilling to listen to history and have therefore pushed all boundaries, structures, values and morals to one side as an outmoded view. As we get alongside young people facing problems, there are no easy answers and certainly no quick fixes. When we look at Jesus' life we see Christianity in its rawest form. It is messy, unpredictable and hands on. Raw Christianity is what is needed on the streets as we encounter desperate young people that have become adrift in a society that no longer seems to care.

> When we look at Jesus, life we see Christianity in its rawest form. It is messy, unpredictable and hands-on.

There have been a lot of positive steps taken in recent years in legislation that protects young people. The main aspect of this is the requirement for all voluntary organisations working with young people to have a Child Protection Policy, relating to protecting the young people that they work with. However in many cases this is not adequate for use in detached work due to the nature of the work and environment. This will mean you may need to review a church policy, for example, and adapt it accordingly. There are other issues that need to be considered, and policies drawn up to protect both the worker and the young person. We have to deal with some issues which the church may not have fully thought through. This is uncharted territory. When we think about our practice we need to be aware of Child Protection, staff safety policy and working philosophy, confidentiality policy, and policies relating to prostitution, theft and violence.

Confidentiality

Confidentiality is an issue in all forms of youth work and it may be that a policy already exists within your setting. In detached work, there are two ways of looking at the issue. The first is the maintenance of total confidentiality between the worker and the young person unless there is a legal requirement to tell a third party, eg Social Services in cases of abuse. This places far more responsibility on the shoulders of the individual and relies heavily on their ability to make professional judgements. It positively empowers young people as it puts the young person first, and they work through the situation, with the worker's support. Within the statutory system you would rarely find a total confidentiality policy, and so, when a young person discloses (or tries to disclose) information this is generally passed on to line managers or other agencies. In the voluntary sector, we do not have those boundaries and so could operate a total confidentiality policy, although we still have a responsibility, through the Criminal Justice Act, to make information available to the police.

The second approach is to have an open confidentiality policy, where issues are shared within the team and with other professional agencies, but no further. Interagency work can be very effective and it can be helpful to discuss cases with other agencies working with the same young people. It is, however, important to respect the wishes of the young person, relating to the information shared.

In detached work you are mainly working as team, and as such, I would advocate a policy that reflects this and takes the best aspects of the two approaches. Confidentiality can be maintained within the team rather than resting with the individual worker, unless there is a legal duty to inform a third party or a worker is subpoenaed. This releases individuals from the weight of an issue that can be better carried by the team as a whole. The wishes of the young person should be upheld wherever possible and they should be informed of the team policy before disclosures are made. This may seem unrealistic, but if we use our common sense we can tell when a young person is about to disclose some important or sensitive issue. They will probably not blurt it out in the middle of a game of football, for example, but try to get the worker to one side and say something like 'Can I tell you something?' perhaps adding, 'You can't tell anyone else'. At this point it is important to explain that you may have to tell someone else, but that normally the matter is only shared with your co-workers, unless it is about abuse. These people should be named so that the young person is fully aware of who you mean. You can further reassure them of this, but offer them the opportunity not to tell you if they are not happy with this.

Where the team feels the need to refer the case on, eg in a case of neglect, efforts should be made to make the young person aware of the situation and where possible work with them to a point of consensus, adhering to your church's or organisation's referral guidelines. There are various other issues that need to be covered by a confidentiality policy, such as how written information is maintained and stored. If a worker is subpoenaed by a court, it is important to work through the issues surrounding whether or not they wish to provide evidence or not, and the consequences of not doing so.

It is important to realise we are not alone. There are many other specialist agencies that can offer information and support. Your community profile may have highlighted some agencies in the area. When referring young people to another agency it is important to include them in the process and discuss each step with them. Passing a young person on to another agency does not relieve you of your responsibility to that person. It may be helpful to go with the young person. You should seek to build up a network of contacts to refer young people on to. This may include a drug agency, a counselling service, a homeless project, a lawyer, a doctor who is not in the area, and a sexual health clinic. Where possible, visit these places and try to get to know someone there who is sympathetic to the aims of your project. Check out their confidentiality procedures, explain your aims and find out what provision can be made out of normal hours.

Paperwork

Keeping a record of your detached work sessions is essential. It enables you to keep track of where you've been, reminds you of names and events and may protects you if questions are asked. There are two types of record that should be kept for used in detached work. The first is a general diary that should be kept for every session. This is a record of general information relating to the session. It should contain information on: the location worked in, date and time of session, workers present, weather, contacts made with young people and other members of the community. A general description of the evening, with issues raised and future action to be taken should be included. Reflection is an important technique in youth work. It helps workers recognise recurring issues, personal weakness, and track the history of contacts, helping maintain a clear perspective in the current situation. So much information is passed on, with so many things happening over a long period of time, that making notes is an essential tool in detached work.

The second type of record is an incident form. These forms should contain more detail, and are used when a dangerous or illegal situation has occurred during a session. The aim of the incident form is to record in detail the incident, the action taken by the young people, the response of the worker and the motivation behind that response. The form helps to protect the worker if their action is later questioned. For example, an incident form would have been completed when the rugby post fell on the child. It would have outlined the situation, and Phil's reasoning for taking the action he did.

We encounter surprising situations on the streets and there will be people in the area that are not supportive of your project. It is essential we act responsibly and professionally and take steps to protect ourselves as well as the young people.

Exploring the edges

● You enter a group and soon discover that they are openly taking drugs: what do you do?

● In what situation might a Christian worker feel they were justified in handing out a condom to a young person? Discuss what you think Jesus would do. What difference might it make if the young person was under 16?

● What evidence can you find that Jesus did or did not practise harm reduction?

Conclusion

Conclusion

Detached youth work can be one of the most rewarding as well as challenging aspects of youth work and ministry. It shouldn't be undertaken lightly, and a long term commitment is essential if the communities we live in and the young people we work with are to benefit from the process.

A letter from an irate local resident to a local paper poured scorn on local young people who vandalized a purpose-built youth shelter. The angry resident demanded a banning of all future service provision for young people and called for heavy penalties for those involved. His basic argument was that the young people of today deserved nothing, because they were so bad.

This view of young people is shared by many. Crime is rising, particularly street crime, and many older people live in fear of younger people. Drug abuse is on the increase and the consequences of teenage alcohol problems can be witnessed in many communities. At the same time, the church has lost vast numbers of young people and urgently needs to rediscover its love for the young people in our communities.

Working with young people on a detached basis will help address all these issues. Perhaps it is time to make a significant investment of time and finance in working in this way. Rather than withdrawing all services for young people (as suggested by Mr Angry), we need rather to provide more opportunities for young people to effectively engage in the community.

The challenge is on for the church to lead the way in this regard. Those faith communities who have taken such steps have really helped the young people they are working with in so many ways. Additionally, such faith groups have been respected and upheld by other members of the community, as beacons of hope for what they are doing.

Churches are increasingly being appreciated for the work they do with young people. They are valued by the local council, police, health workers, youth workers and parents alike. They are truly taking their place at the heart of the communities they live in.

This is of course, a by-product of detached youth work. The main purpose is to build effective and empowering relationships with marginalised young people, who are often facing social exclusion, a life of disengagement and crime and low levels of hope and aspiration.

Detached youth work seems to embrace kingdom values on many levels and seeks to minister in the same way that Jesus did. If you are up for the challenge and want to make a significant difference in the lives of the young people in your community, I can think of few better ways than developing a detached youth work project to work alongside any existing projects.

Appendix A

Summary of general guidelines for detached work

1   **a** As a general rule it is expected that workers should work in pairs. Initially the pairs would be a team leader and a volunteer, but once trained it is acceptable for two volunteers to work together.

    b A team leader or key worker may be able to work individually if:
- the situation requires it.
- there is an established ongoing relationship with the young person being contacted.
- the worker is carrying a mobile phone and has change for a public telephone
- the worker stays in sight of other members of the team.

    c All individual work must be agreed beforehand with the project manager.

2   Team members should always be aware of other members of the team, their whereabouts, and actions.

3   At all times workers must:
    a carry their ID cards.
    b carry a mobile phone and change for a public phone.

4   Confidentiality policies and codes of conduct should be followed at all times

5   Aggressive behaviour should never be returned with aggression.

6   **a** A general record sheet should always be completed by the whole team at the end of the session.

    b Fifteen minutes should be taken at the end of each session for evaluation and to complete the record sheet.

7   **a** Should an incident arise, an incident record should also be made. Incidents to be recorded include: drug use, theft

(suspected or otherwise) knowledge of illegal activity, child abuse, an accident or injury to a young person or worker, or an issue that the worker feels may put them at risk of further repercussion.

b If a third party (eg the emergency services) is called as a result of an incident, or an assault is made on a worker, then a trustee or member of the management team must be called to attend the site to support the worker.

8 **a** Avoid physical contact wherever possible.

b Avoid *all* physical contact with the opposite sex.

9 Only use the car in exceptional circumstances. Valid reasons must be given for a lift. Lifts must only be given if the car/driver is suitably insured. If unsure of the policy, decline lifts.

10 **a** Seek to maintain positive relationships between team members whilst young people are present. Avoid arguments and disagreements while young people are present.

b Do not discuss cases in front of other young people, or enter into negative conversations about a young person with other young people.

c It is appropriate to spend time with a small group. Do not feel pressured to meet everyone every week.

d Ensure work with a small group is consolidated before trying to mix it with another established group.

11 Ensure prayer takes place prior to the session and follow this up with prayer in your own time.

12 **a** Do not lend money except in exceptional circumstances. It may be appropriate to lend money as a trust issue.

b We recognise that from time to time it is valid to buy refreshments when working individually or in small groups.

Training recommendations

Before commencing detached work, a worker should receive training which includes:

Building relationships

Community profiles, if starting a new project, and yearly afterwards

Harm reduction

Confidentiality

Procedures and guidelines

Child Protection

Cold contact

Making records

Action to be taken when approaching illegal activity

Introduction to informal education and exploring faith with non-churched young people.

Within 6–12 months of their appointment, workers should receive further training on:

Informal education

Team work principles and leading teams

Young people's spiritual development.

After 12 months, training should be given on:

Non-book culture

Integrating young people into churches

Developing worship initiatives with young people.

Suggested guidelines for management group/trustees when attending a detached site

- Attend the site if you are requested to by a worker.

- Ensure that the incident sheet has been completed, and sign it if it is appropriate.

- Ensure the emotional, spiritual, and physical well-being of all workers involved before leaving the site.

- Agree any follow-up support or action to be taken, with the team leader.

- Ensure the confidentiality of the incident within the team and follow confidentiality guidelines.

- Contact the director or detached team leader on the evening if possible, or as soon as possible after the event, ideally within 24 hours.

Appendix B

Sample outline of schools-based detached project

Aim

To form positive relationships with young people, providing a role model with whom they can identify closely and share their problems and aspirations with.

Worker's role

When working with pupils, the worker should do the following.

● Present themselves as a non-authoritarian figure.

Be a confidant.

Offer support to those on the edge of the school community.

Offer informal counselling.

Identify specific difficulties, and help the young people to overcome them.

Encourage participation in extra curricular activities.

When working with staff, the worker should do the following.

Have a specific staff member as a contact, to deal with any staff enquiries.

Be available once a week for staff as an adult helper.

Be available for staff to refer a young person to.

Be a resource to the school.

Be available for school residentials and activity weeks.

Each school will have particular needs and expectations, and the worker must liaise with staff about issues such as confidentiality, times to work in school, and frequency of visits. The worker should remember that they are not in the school to proselytise, but to share themselves as part of their faith.

Appendix C

Sample Job Description

Job Title: Detached and Schools Project Worker

Purpose: To take our detached work project forward in (*Suchatown*). The project seeks to engage with hard to reach and marginalised young people, with a view to helping them find a place within the local community. The purpose of this post is to implement the project and ensure it achieves its aims. In addition, the worker will have responsibility for advising a group of young people in our Youth Award scheme, who are struggling to remain in mainstream education.

Accountability: The post holder will be responsible to the Project Coordinator for (*ABC Organisation*).

Responsibility: The post holder will be responsible for the recruitment, training and leading of a team of volunteers to develop a detached youth work project in (*Suchatown*). The post holder will be responsible for liaising with other agencies in the area who work with young people. A large proportion of the post holder's time will be spent in direct work with the young people with whom contact has been made on the streets.

Main Functions: The post holder will be responsible for liaising with local church leaders and the local Christian community to ensure the project is understood and supported and in order to recruit volunteers to assist in the work.

The post holder will take responsibility in leading sessions of detached youth work in (*Suchatown*) identifying and engaging with marginalized and disaffected young people.

The post holder will make contact with, build knowledge of and develop professional and working relationships with other local agencies including the police, the local youth service, teachers and learning mentors, in order to promote the work of the project and in order to ensure that young people are able to take their place within the community.

The post holder will ensure that all relevant policies are implemented throughout any work carried out including Health and Safety policy and Child Protection policy.

The post holder will develop a youth award programme and an informal education programme in secondary schools or other less formal learning environments in (*Suchatown*), meeting regularly with identified groups of young people, and encouraging them to work towards the Bronze Youth Award.

- The post holder should hold regular meetings with school staff to ensure the effectiveness of this programme.

- The post holder will write regular reviews and reports on the development of the project for the Local Management Group and for those funding the programme.

- The post holder will take part in staff meetings and contribute to the overall development and strategy of (*ABC Organisation*).

- The post holder will meet regularly with the Project Coordinator actively contributing to informal and formal supervision and support.

- The post holder will contribute to forthcoming funding bids in particular relating to the detached youth work project.

Relationships: The post holder will have regular contact with the (*Suchatown*) Project Coordinator for (*ABC Organisation*) and other (*ABC Organisation*) staff and volunteers. The existing team support and encourage one another, but there is also an expectation that workers operate with a high level of independence and autonomy. Project workers are expected to plan and manage their own workload, using their own skills and initiative.

Working Hours: This is a 20 hour per week post, to be worked in a flexible manner according to the needs of the young people being targeted. Some evening and weekend work can be expected and there is also a likelihood at some time that the post holder will take part in residential trips.

Performance Indicators: A number of performance targets for work with young people have been set within the funding bids and these will need to be adhered to.

Terms and Conditions:

4 weeks holiday to be taken out of school term time.

Additional job conditions and terms of employment continue here, depending on legal situation and pre-existing working practice.

References

[1] Mayo B, *Gospel Exploded* (Triangle, SPCK, 1996), p12

[2] Passmore R and Hawes J, *Streetwork Skills and Knowhow* (Realise the Future, 1994), p4

[3] Friere P, *Pedagogy of the Oppressed* (SCM Press, 1982), pvii

[4] Mountain A, ed. *Understanding Detached Work and Helping Others Manage it* (National Youth Bureau, 1989)

[5] Sheppard L, *Strategy for the 90's* (Youth for Christ, 1993), p3 *(nb This was the YFC strategy for the 90's, not the current strategy)*

[6] Thatcher M, October 1987

[7] Bartlett R, *Future Trends in Youth Ministry* (Youth for Christ, 1997)

[8] Evangelical Urban Training Project Handout 1992

[9] Ward P, *Growing up Evangelical: Youthwork and the Making of a Sub Culture* (SPCK, 1996)

[10] Groves J, *Unchurching the churched* (Diocese of Gloucester, 1997)

[11] Donovan V, *Christianity Rediscovered: An Epistle from the Masai* (second edition) (SCM Press Ltd, 1982) p vii

[12] Kreidar A, *Journey Towards Holiness: A Way of Living for God's Nation* (Herald Press, 1987)

[13] Harm reduction definition adapted from training session by Gloucestershire Drugs Project 1994

Other informative books

Breen M, *Outside In* (SU, 1993)

Church of England, *Youth Apart* (Church House, 1996)

Fearon M, *With God on the Frontiers* (SU, 1989)

Ong W, *Orality and Literature* (Routledge, 1982)

Pimlott J, Pimlott N and Wiles D, *Inspire* (SU, 2002)

Riddell M, *Threshold of the Future* (SPCK, 1998)

Sine T, *Wild Hope* (World Publishing, 1991)

Twelvetrees A, *Community Work* (Palgrave Macmillan, 1982)

Ward P, *Gospel and Youth Culture* (Zondervan, 1992)

Wink W, *Transforming Bible Study* (Abingdon Press,1989)

Xcelerate:

The evangelist's heartbeat

Matt Wilson and Andy Hawthorne

Luis Palau says, 'Only touch this book if you don't mind getting scorched!' Why? Well, it features valuable lessons from well-known evangelists and down to earth stories from the street. A straight talking manual to help you think clearly about spreading the message of Christ, produced together with Manchester's pioneering Message Trust.

B Format 192pp £6.99

ISBN 1 85999 607 8

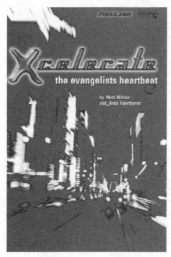

Inspire!:

Fresh ideas for creative youth work

Nigel Pimlott, Jo Pimlott and Dave Wiles

Inspiring youth work is not about lecturing or nagging – it's about making it possible for young people to develop and own their ideas and choices about life and faith.

Share in the experiences and visions of leading youth workers as they suggest general principles to help with group work, creativity and real participation. The accompanying CD ROM contains over 100 activities for use in different church and youth group situations, including photocpiable worksheets.

B Format 80pp and CD ROM £14.99

ISBN 1 85999 429 6